ATDD by Example

ATDD by Example

A Practical Guide to Acceptance Test-Driven Development

Markus Gärtner

✦✦ Addison-Wesley

Upper Saddle River, NJ • Boston • Indianapolis • San Francisco
New York • Toronto • Montreal • London • Munich • Paris • Madrid
Capetown • Sydney • Tokyo • Singapore • Mexico City

Many of the designations used by manufacturers and sellers to distinguish their products are claimed as trademarks. Where those designations appear in this book, and the publisher was aware of a trademark claim, the designations have been printed with initial capital letters or in all capitals.

The author and publisher have taken care in the preparation of this book, but make no expressed or implied warranty of any kind and assume no responsibility for errors or omissions. No liability is assumed for incidental or consequential damages in connection with or arising out of the use of the information or programs contained herein.

The publisher offers excellent discounts on this book when ordered in quantity for bulk purchases or special sales, which may include electronic versions and/or custom covers and content particular to your business, training goals, marketing focus, and branding interests. For more information, please contact:

U.S. Corporate and Government Sales
(800) 382-3419
corpsales@pearsontechgroup.com

For sales outside the United States, please contact:

International Sales
international@pearson.com

Visit us on the Web: informit.com/aw

Library of Congress Cataloging-in-Publication Data

Gärtner, Markus, 1979-
  ATDD by example / Markus Gärtner.
    p. cm.
  Includes bibliographical references and index.
  ISBN-10: 0-321-78415-4 (pbk. : alk. paper)
  ISBN-13: 978-0-321-78415-5 (pbk. : alk. paper)
  1. Agile software development - Case studies. 2. Automation. 3. Systems engineering. I. Title.
  QA76.76.D47G374 2013
  005.1–dc23   2012016163

ISBN-13: 978-0-321-78415-5
ISBN-10:   0-321-78415-4
Text printed in the United States on recycled paper at Courier in Westford, Massachusetts.
First printing, July 2012

To my wife Jennifer, my pet-son Leon, and our daughter Katrin,
who allowed me to spend way too little time
with them while writing this.

Contents

Foreword

by Kent Beck

There is a curious symmetry to the way this book presents Acceptance Test-Driven Development and the way software is developed with ATDD. Just as there is an art to picking the specific examples of program behavior that will elicit the correct general behavior for the system, there is an art to picking specific examples of a programming technique like ATDD to give you, the reader, a chance to learn the technique for yourself. Markus has done an admirable job in selecting and presenting examples.

To read this book you will need to read code. If you follow along, you will have the opportunity to learn the shift in thinking that is required to succeed with ATDD. That shift is, in short, to quickly go from, "Here's a feature I'd like," to "How are we going to test that? Here's an example." Reading the examples, you will see, over and over, what that transition looks like in various contexts.

What I like about this code-centric presentation is the trust it shows in your powers of learning. This isn't "12 Simple Rules for Testing Your Web App" printed on intellectual tissue paper that falls apart at first contact with the moisture of reality. Here you will read about concrete decisions made in concrete contexts, decisions that you could (and that, if you want to get the most out of this book, you will) disagree with, debate, and decide for yourself.

The latter portions of the book do draw general conclusions, summarizing the principles at work in the examples. If you are someone who learns more efficiently when you are familiar with general concepts, that will be a good place to start. Regardless, what you get out of this book is directly proportional to the investment you are willing to make in following the examples.

One of the weaknesses of TDD as originally described is that it can devolve into a programmer's technique used to meet a programmer's needs. Some programmers take a broader view of TDD, facilely shifting between levels of abstraction for their tests. However, with ATDD there is no ambiguity—this is a technique for enhancing communication with people for whom programming languages are foreign. The quality of our relationships, and the communication that underlies those relationships, encourages effective software development. ATDD can be used to take a step in the direction of clearer communication, and *ATDD by Example* is a thorough, approachable introduction.

–Kent Beck

Foreword
by Dale Emery

Too many software projects fail to deliver what their customers request. Over the years, I've heard scores of project customers explain the failures: *The developers don't pay attention to what we ask them to build.* And I've heard hundreds of developers explain the failures: *The customers don't tell us what they want. Most of the time they don't even know what they want.*

I've observed enough projects to come to a different conclusion: Describing a software system's responsibilities is hard. It requires speaking and listening with precision that is rare—and rarely so necessary—in normal human interactions. Writing good software is hard. Testing software well is hard. But the hardest job in software is communicating clearly about what we want the system to do.

Acceptance Test-Driven Development (ATDD) helps with the challenge. Using ATDD, the whole team collaborates to gain clarity and shared understanding before development begins. At the heart of ATDD are two key practices: Before implementing each feature, team members collaborate to create concrete examples of the feature in action. Then the team translates these examples into automated acceptance tests. These examples and tests become a prominent part of the team's shared, precise description of "done" for each feature.

What is shared understanding worth? One developer at an ATDD workshop explained it this way: "Once we started to work together to create examples, I started to *care* about the work we were doing. I finally understood what we were building and why. Even more importantly, I knew that the whole team understood what we were trying to accomplish. Suddenly we all had the same goal—we were all on the same team."

ATDD helps us not only to know when we're done, but also to know when we're making progress. As we automate each test and write the software that passes the test (and all of the previous tests), the examples serve as signposts along the road to completion. And because each example describes a responsibility that customers value, we can have confidence that not only are we making progress, we're making progress that matters.

Okay, I've listed a few of ATDD's key features and a few of its key benefits. That's the easy part. As for the heavy lifting: How do you actually do this stuff so that it works in the real world? I'll leave that to Markus Gärtner. In *ATDD by Example*, Markus rolls up his sleeves and not only tells you but *shows* you how ATDD works in practice. He lets you peek over the shoulders and into the minds of testers, programmers, and business experts as they apply the principles and practices of ATDD.

I offer one caveat as you read this book: The first few chapters—in which we follow business expert Bill, tester Tony, and programmers Phyllis and Alex as they describe and implement a small software system—may seem at first glance to be overly simple, or even simplistic. Don't be fooled by that appearance. There is a *lot* going on in these chapters. This is a skilled team, and some of their skills are subtle. Notice, for example, that in the requirements workshop the team members avoid any mention of technology. They focus entirely on the system's business responsibilities. And notice that as Alex and Tony automate the first few tests, Tony makes good use of his *lack* of programming experience. Whenever he is confused by some technical detail, he asks Alex to explain, and then works with Alex to edit the code so that the code explains itself. And notice how frequently Alex insists on checking the tests into the source control system—but only when the code is working. If you're new to ATDD, these skills may not be obvious, but they're essential to success.

Fortunately, all you need to do to learn about these subtle skills is to keep reading. Markus pauses frequently to explain what the team is doing and why. At the end of each chapter he summarizes how the team worked together, what they were thinking, and the practices they applied. And in the final portion of the book, Markus brings it all together by describing in detail the principles that make ATDD work.

ATDD by Example is a great introduction to Acceptance Test-Driven Development. It also offers a fresh perspective for people like me who have been practicing ATDD for a while. Finally, it is a book that rewards multiple readings. So read, practice, and read again. You'll learn something new and useful each time.

–Dale Emery

Preface

In this book I give an entry-level introduction to the practice that has become known as Acceptance Test-Driven Development—or ATDD. When I first came across the term ATDD in 2008, I assumed that it was artificial and unnecessary. It seemed superfluous to me as I had learned test-driven development in 2008 and found it sufficient. In the end, why would I need to test for acceptance criteria?

"Time wounds all heels" [Wei86]. So, four years later I find myself writing a book on what has become known as Acceptance Test-Driven Development. Throughout 2009 I ran into Gojko Adzic, who had just finished his book *Bridging the Communication Gap* [Adz09]. He gave me a copy of that book, and I immediately started to read it on my way back from London. Once I had finished it, I had a good understanding about what ATDD is and why we should avoid that name.

But why did I still use the name *ATDD by Example* for the paper stack you hold in your hands?[1]

On the Name

ATDD has been around for some time now. It is known by different terms. Here is an incomplete list:

- Acceptance Test-Driven Development
- Behavior-Driven Development (BDD)
- Specification by Example
- Agile Acceptance Testing
- Story Testing

---

1. Or, why did I use the particular arrangement of 1s and 0s that displays as "ATDD by Example" on your electronic device?

From my perspective, any of these names comes with a drawback. Acceptance Test-Driven Development creates the notion that we are finished with the iteration once the acceptance tests pass. This is not true, because with any selection of tests, the coverage is incomplete. There are gaps in the net of tests. In the testing world, this is well known as the impossibility to test everything. Instead we know exactly we are not finished when an acceptance test fails—as Michael Bolton put it.

Despite arguing for one name or another, I decided to put a selection of possible alternatives here and have the readers decide which fits best their need. In the end it does not matter to me what you call it, as long as it's working for you. The world of software development is full of misleading terms and probably will stay so for some more years. Software engineering, test automation, test-driven development are all misleading in one way or another. As with any abstraction, don't confuse the name for the thing. The expert knows the limitations of the name of the approach.

But why have there been different names for a similar approach? The practices you use may very well differ. Having visited and consulted multiple teams in multiple companies on ATDD, they all have one thing in common: Each team is different from the others. While one practice might work for your team in your current company, it might fail dramatically in another. Have you ever wondered about the answer "it depends" from a consultant? This is the source of it.

For his book *Specification by Example* [Adz11], Gojko Adzic interviewed more than fifty teams that apply ATDD in one form or another. What he found is a variety of practices accompanying the ATDD approach. All of the teams that apply ATDD successfully start with a basic approach, then revisit it after some time, and adapt some changes in order to fit their particular context. Starting with a lightweight process and adapting new things as you find problems is a very agile way of implementing any approach. As you apply ATDD, keep in mind that your first set of practices is unlikely to solve all your problems. Over time you will adapt the solution process as you gain more and more experience.

Why Another Book on ATDD?

While Gojko describes many patterns of successful ATDD implementations, I found there is a major gap in the books on ATDD up until now. There is a considerable difference between advanced adopters of a skill or approach and entry-level demands for the same skill or approach.

When going through the literature on ATDD, I found several books that explain ATDD on an advanced level by referring to principles. For an advanced learner, it is easy to apply principles in their particular context. However, this does not hold for a novice on the same topic. A novice needs more concrete directions in order to get started. Once a person gains experience with the basics, he or she can start to break free from the hard constraints of the approach.

Novices learn best by following a recipe, but by no means is this book a cookbook on ATDD. With the examples in this book, I provide two working approaches to ATDD and expose the thought processes of the people involved. The novice learner can use these to get started with ATDD on her team. As we go along, I provide pointers to more in-depth material.

The basic idea is taken from Kent Beck's *Test-Driven Development: By Example* [Bec02]. Beck provides two working examples on Test-Driven Development and explains some of the principles behind it in the end. It is intended as an entry-level description of TDD and provides the novice with enough learning material to get started—assuming that through reflection and practice TDD can be learned. The same holds true to some degree for this book as well.

Vocabulary

Throughout the book I will use several terms from the Agile software development world. Realizing that not everyone knows about Agile software development, a brief introduction of some terms is in place.

Product Owner In the Agile method Scrum three roles are defined: the development team, the ScrumMaster, and the Product Owner. The Product Owner is responsible for the success of the product that the team will build. He or she sets priorities for the features that the team will be implementing and works together with other stakeholders to derive them. He or she is also the customer representative for the team and decides about details in that function—and has to negotiate with the other stakeholders about this.

Iteration, or Sprint Agile development relies on a regular cycle called the iteration or Sprint in Scrum. These are short bursts where the team implements a single product increment that is potentially shippable. Common iteration lengths vary between one and four weeks.

User Story A user story is a limited set of functionality that the team feels comfortable implementing over the course of a single iteration. These are tiny slices through the functionality. Usually a team strives to implement several user stories in one iteration. The business representative or product owner is responsible for defining these stories.

Taskboard Most Agile teams plan their work on a board visually accessible to anyone. They use cards to indicate what they are working on. The taskboard usually has several columns, at least ToDo, Doing, and Done. As the work proceeds, the team updates the taskboard to reflect this.

Story Card User stories are usually written on real cards. During the iteration, the cards are put onto the team's taskboard.

Standup Meeting, Daily Scrum At least once per day team members update themselves on the current state of the iteration. The team gets together for 15 minutes and discusses how they can finish currently open tasks until the end of the iteration.

Product Backlog, Sprint Backlog The Product Owner in Scrum organizes unimplemented stories in a product backlog. He or she is responsible for updating the backlog whenever new requirements enter. When the team gets together to plan the next sprint, the team members identify a backlog for the next sprint length. This is called the Sprint Backlog. The selected stories from the Product Backlog automatically become part of the Sprint Backlog. The Sprint Backlog is most often organized on the taskboard after the planning meeting.

Refactoring Refactoring is changing the structure of the source code without changing what it does. Usually I refactor code before introducing changes. By refactoring my code I make the task of implementing the upcoming changes more easy.

Test-Driven Development (TDD) In test-driven development you write one single test that fails, write just enough code that makes this failing test pass (and all the other passing tests still pass), and then refactor your code to prepare it for the next tiny step. TDD is a design approach, and it helps users write better code, because testable code is written by default.

Continuous Integration (CI) In Continuous Integration you integrate the changes in the source code often. A build server then builds the whole branch, executes all unit tests and all acceptance tests, and spreads the information about this build to your colleagues. CI relies on an automated build, and it helps teams to see problems with the current state of the branch very early—not just one hour before the release shall be shipped.

How to Read This Book

In this book I provide a mixture of concrete practices alongside some of the principles that I found useful. There are multiple ways to read this book—depending on your experience level you may pick any of them.

You may read this book cover to cover. You will get to know more about Cucumber, Behavior-Driven Development and how to test webpages using an ATDD tool. The first example is also based on a team that differentiates between testing experts and programming experts. You will find collabooration as one key success factor there.

In the second part I will pair up with you. By pairing up we can compensate for any missing testing or programming knowledge at this point. We will drive our application code using ATDD in a practical way. We will deal with FitNesse, a wiki-based acceptance test framework. The examples in the second part are covered in Java.

In the third part you will find some guidance on how to get started with the approach. I give pointers to further readings as well as hints on how to get started, what worked well, and what did not work so well for other teams.

In the appendixes you will find the two tools used in this book and even a third one explained in some depth to get you started. If you haven't run into Cucumber or FitNesse, you may want to start there.

An advanced-level reader might skip the first two parts initially and directly start with the principles I explain in the third part. Maybe you want to provide some background to your colleagues later. The examples in Parts I and II serve this purpose.

You may also read the first two examples, and then head back to work to start a basic implementation. Once you reach a dead end, you may come back to read further material in Part III—although I wouldn't necessarily recommend reading this book in this order.

If you already have an ATDD implementation in place on your team, you may want to dig deeper in Part II where I explain how to drive the domain code from your examples.

These are some ways in which I can imagine reading this book. If you're like me, you're probably thinking of following the examples by implementing the provided code on your own. I set up a github repository for each of the code examples. These allowed me to acceptance test the code examples on my own. If you find yourself stuck, you can have a peek there as well. You will find the examples for the first part at http://github.com/mgaertne/airport, and the sources for the second part at http://github.com/mgaertne/trafficlights.

Acknowledgments

A project such as this book would not be possible without the support of so many helpers. First of all, I would like to thank Dale Emery, who provided me great comments on my writing style. Being a non-native English writer, I really appreciated the feedback I got from Dale.

A special thank you goes to Kent Beck. In August 2010 I approached him on the topic of writing a book on ATDD following the approach he used in *TDD by Example*. He also introduced me to Addison-Wesley and to Christopher Guzikowski, who provided me all the support to get this book published.

Several people have provided me feedback on early drafts. For this feedback I thank Lisa Crispin, Matt Heusser, Elisabeth Hendrickson, Brett Schuchert, Gojko Adzic, George Dinwiddie, Kevin Bodie, Olaf Lewitz, Manuel Küblböck, Andreas Havenstein, Sebastian Sanitz, Meike Mertsch, Gregor Gramlich, and Stephan Kämper.

Last, but not least, I would like to thank my wife Jennifer and our children Katrin and Leon for their support while writing this book. I hope to be able to return the time you had to deal without a husband or a dad in the years to come.

About the Author

Markus Gärtner works as an Agile tester, trainer, coach, and consultant with it-agile GmbH, Hamburg, Germany. Markus, a student of the work of Jerry Weinberg, founded the German Agile Testing and Exploratory workshop in 2011 and is one of the founders of the European chapter of Weekend Testing. He is a black-belt instructor in the Miagi-Do school of Software Testing and contributes to the Agile Alliance FTT-Patterns writing community, as well as the Software Craftsmanship movement. Markus regularly presents at Agile and testing conferences all over the globe, as well as dedicating himself to writing about testing, foremost in an Agile context. He maintains a personal blog at shino.de/blog. He teaches ATDD and context-driven testing to customers in the Agile world. He has taught ATDD to testers with a nontechnical background, as well as to several programmers.

Part I

Airport Parking Lot

In this part we will take a look at an online application. Test automation on web pages is one of the things that works quite well through the graphical user interface today. But there are drawbacks to such an approach. However, most teams dealing with online applications will find some hints how to drive their tests in here.

The application to be built is a parking cost calculator for an international airport. There are several parking lots at the airport with different prices for parking durations.

The business rules for the parking cost calculator are complicated enough to make the team fail at the last attempt to build such an online application. Since team members think they got the requirements wrong, they decided to vary their approach this time. The application will be discussed within an Specification Workshop with the customer. Testers, programmers, and customers discuss examples that express the business rules of the parking cost calculator.

In parallel with the programming activities, the tester automates these examples using Cucumber and Ruby in combination with Selenium. At some time he might need help from a programmer on this, but I don't want to reveal too much in the introduction.

Just in case you are wondering what kind of tool the tester Tony is using to edit the Cucumber examples, of course Tony uses emacs, not vi.

Chapter 1

Parking Cost Calculator Workshop

A while ago the Major International Airport Corp. decided to extend its Internet presence. In particular their website should enable potential travelers the option of pre-calculating parking costs. Travelers should be able to fill out an online form that calculates the parking lot costs for their particular choice of travel duration.

Previously Major International Airport Corp. built such a form. The feedback from travelers on the current form is so bad that the management team decided to rewrite it from scratch.

Based on the experiences from the previous project, the implementation team, consisting of one senior programmer, Phyllis, one programmer, Alex, and one tester, Tony, takes a new approach. On the first implementation of the project the requirements seemed to keep changing all the time, resulting in code that was extended with patch after patch, just to find out that the wrong thing was implemented right from the start.

Instead of repeating the process anew, the team uses a specification workshop in order to gather the business rules of the parking lot calculator. In preparation for the new functionality, Phyllis and Tony invite the manager of Major International Airport Corp.'s parking lot division, Bill, as a business expert for parking lot costs to a meeting.

Valet Parking

PHYLLIS OK, then let's discuss the parking lot cost calculation requirements. Bill, what can you tell us about them?

BILL We basically have three types of parking lots. Some have costs per hour, some per day, some have a daily or weekly maximum.

PHYLLIS How do you refer to the different parking lots? Are there names for them?

BILL   Valet parking, short-term parking, and regular parking. If you lose your ticket, you will be charged a fee of $10.00.

PHYLLIS Let's try to concentrate on the three types. What's the difference between them?

BILL   For valet parking, the passenger drops his or her car off at the valet dropoff and gets a receipt to get the car back.

PHYLLIS What can you tell us about parking costs?

BILL   Valet parking costs $18.00 per day. For five hours or less you get a reduction of $6.00.

TONY   Wait a moment, Bill. You mean for even 30 minutes I get charged $12.00, for three hours I have to pay the same, as well as for five hours? But for five hours and one minute I have to pay $18.00 as well as for twelve or even twenty-four hours?

BILL   Yes, absolutely right.

TONY   What about twenty-four hours and one minute? Would this be $30.00 then, or $36.00?

BILL   Oh, that is of course $36.00.

PHYLLIS What about weekly limits? Are there any for valet parking?

BILL   No, that's basically all there is for valet parking.

TONY   OK, then let me write these down as examples.

Tony writes down Table 1.1 representing the discussed examples and labels it "Valet Parking."

PHYLLIS Are these examples meaningful for valet parking?

BILL   Yes, these sum up our conversation.

Table 1.1 Initial Valet Parking Examples

Parking Duration	Parking Costs
30 minutes	$12.00
3 hours	$12.00
5 hours	$12.00
5 hours 1 minute	$18.00
12 hours	$18.00
24 hours	$18.00
1 day 1 minute	$36.00
3 days	$54.00
1 week	$126.00

Short-Term Parking

PHYLLIS OK, what other type of parking costs are there? You mentioned three different types.

BILL We also offer short-term parking places for visitors dropping off or picking up other passengers.

PHYLLIS How much does that cost?

BILL We charge $2.00 for the first hour. Then for each half hour it's another $1.00.

TONY Is there any boundary such as maximum parking duration?

BILL No, there isn't. Although we charge just up to $24.00 per single day.

PHYLLIS So, we have a daily maximum of $24.00?

BILL Right.

TONY And after the first day the first hour will be charged at $2.00, or does it increase the costs then on a half-hour basis?

BILL Oh, it's a $25.00 for one day and half an hour.

TONY What about a weekly maximum? Is there one?

BILL No. For short-term parking people won't stay a week, since it's probably too expensive for them. The third option is way more attractive.

TONY OK, what do you think about this table?

Tony has written down Table 1.2 and shares it with Bill and Phyllis.

BILL Yes, that's it, exactly.

Table 1.2 Initial Short-Term Parking Examples

Parking Duration	Parking Costs
30 minutes	$2.00
1 hour	$2.00
1 hour 30 minutes	$3.00
2 hours	$4.00
3 hours 30 minutes	$7.00
12 hours	$24.00
12 hours 30 minutes	$24.00
1 day 30 minutes	$25.00
1 day 1 hour	$26.00

Economy and Long-Term Parking

PHYLLIS Now, what's the third type of parking costs that we will need to calculate?

BILL There is also economy parking. The lot is placed way apart from the airport. That's what makes it cheaper for the passengers. We have a bus shuttle to get travelers to the terminal.

PHYLLIS All right, how cheap is it?

BILL The rules are a bit more complicated there. First, parking costs $2.00 per hour.

TONY Any day? Or do you charge a different fee maybe for the weekends?

BILL No, the day of week does not matter.

TONY So, in the Economy Lot the first 30 minutes as well as the first 60 minutes cost exactly $2.00, right?

BILL Exactly.

PHYLLIS Well, that does not sound complicated. Three hours then probably cost $6.00 while ten hours would cost $20.00.

BILL Yes, and no. We have a daily maximum of $9.00. That means that the first hour to the fourth hour will be charged at $2.00 each. The fifth hour then raises the costs to the daily maximum of $9.00. Any additional hour does not raise the costs until the next day.

TONY So, we have half hour, one hour, $2.00, three hours $6.00, four hours $8.00, five hours $9.00, six hours $9.00, twenty-four hours $9.00. . .

BILL Yes, that sounds fine with me.

TONY OK, what happens on the second day? Do we add $2.00, or do we add $9.00 then on a daily basis?

BILL No, it's then another $2.00 added to the sum per hour, up to a daily maximum of $9.00 again.

TONY So, one day and half an hour costs $11.00, one day and five hours $18.00. And I suppose that the third, fourth, fifth, . . . is just like that?

BILL Yes, but there is yet another limitation. There is a weekly maximum of up to $54.00. So, basically the seventh day is free of charge.

TONY OK, I got that. Let me sum this up. Here is the table I created while we were talking.

Tony shows Bill and Phyllis Table 1.3, which he labeled "Economy Parking."

BILL Yes, that looks good.

PHYLLIS Wait a minute, Bill. What about six days and one hour? Does that sum up to $56.00 or rather $54.00?

Table 1.3 Initial Economy Parking Examples

Parking Duration	Parking Costs
30 minutes	$2.00
1 hour	$2.00
3 hours	$6.00
4 hours	$8.00
5 hours	$9.00
6 hours	$9.00
24 hours	$9.00
1 day, 1 hour	$11.00
1 day, 3 hours	$15.00
1 day, 5 hours	$18.00
3 days	$27.00
6 days	$54.00
7 days	$54.00
1 week, 2 days	$72.00
3 weeks	$162.00

BILL   No, that's still $54.00 since the seventh day is free of charge. But maybe we should add that example as well.

TONY   I added it already.

PHYLLIS   All right, that's all there is to parking lot costs then?

BILL   No, there are two variations of Economy Parking. For parking long-term in the garage, parking costs are $2.00 per hour, $12.00 as daily maximum, and the seventh day is free as well. For long-term parking without the garage we charge $2.00 per hour, with a daily maximum of $10.00, and the seventh day is free here, too.

TONY   So, do these two tables reflect this?

Tony has created Tables 1.4 and 1.5 and shows them to Bill and Phyllis.

BILL   Yeah, this looks good.

PHYLLIS   One more concern. Regarding the twenty-four-hour example, what happens if we arrive at 11 pm and stay until the next day 11 pm? Does this yield one day plus the second day, each $10.00, so a total of $20.00?

BILL   No, we will charge $10.00 since the overall parking duration has been twenty-four hours.

TONY   Is this the same handling for multiple days in the parking lot?

BILL   Absolutely. The day boundary does not matter in all cases, just the boundary in the overall parking duration.

Table 1.4 Initial Long-Term Garage
Parking Examples

Parking Duration	Parking Costs
30 minutes	$2.00
1 hour	$2.00
3 hours	$6.00
6 hours	$12.00
7 hours	$12.00
24 hours	$12.00
1 day, 1 hour	$14.00
1 day, 3 hours	$18.00
1 day, 7 hours	$24.00
3 days	$36.00
6 days	$72.00
6 days, 1 hour	$72.00
7 days	$72.00
1 week, 2 days	$96.00
3 weeks	$216.00

Table 1.5 Initial Long-Term Surface
Parking Examples

Parking Duration	Parking Costs
30 minutes	$2.00
1 hour	$2.00
3 hours	$6.00
4 hours	$8.00
5 hours	$10.00
6 hours	$10.00
24 hours	$10.00
1 day, 1 hour	$12.00
1 day, 3 hours	$16.00
1 day, 6 hours	$20.00
3 days	$30.00
6 days	$60.00
6 days, 1 hour	$60.00
7 days	$60.00
1 week, 2 days	$80.00
3 weeks	$180.00

Essential Examples

TONY   Now, we are nearly finished. There is one final step we have to do with all these examples. I think we understand the business requirements, but I would like to reduce the number of examples now to reflect the essence of the business rules. Let's go over the tables one last time and see what we can and should throw out.

BILL   Let's work backwards. I would like to drop some of the long-term surface parking examples.

Bill strikes through some of the examples from the long-term surface parking table. The results are shown in Table 1.6.

PHYLLIS What about the three days example? We already have one and six days covered. May we drop this one as well?

TONY   Yes, probably. Bill, what do you think?

BILL   Yeah, let's drop it. We have pretty much everything covered there. I think it's safe to drop that one as well.

Table 1.6 Long-Term Surface Parking Examples After Bill Removed Some Redundant Examples

Parking Duration	Parking Costs
30 minutes	$2.00
1 hour	$2.00
~~3 hours~~	~~$6.00~~
~~4 hours~~	~~$8.00~~
5 hours	$10.00
6 hours	$10.00
24 hours	$10.00
1 day, 1 hour	$12.00
1 day, 3 hours	$16.00
1 day, 6 hours	$20.00
3 days	$30.00
6 days	$60.00
6 days, 1 hour	$60.00
7 days	$60.00
1 week, 2 days	$80.00
3 weeks	$180.00

Table 1.7 Long-Term Surface Parking Examples
After Bill Removed Redundant Examples

Parking Duration	Parking Costs
30 minutes	$2.00
1 hour	$2.00
~~3 hours~~	~~$6.00~~
~~4 hours~~	~~$8.00~~
5 hours	$10.00
6 hours	$10.00
24 hours	$10.00
1 day, 1 hour	$12.00
1 day, 3 hours	$16.00
1 day, 6 hours	$20.00
~~3 days~~	~~$30.00~~
6 days	$60.00
6 days, 1 hour	$60.00
7 days	$60.00
1 week, 2 days	$80.00
3 weeks	$180.00

Table 1.7 shows the cleaned up examples.

BILL   For long-term garage parking, I think it's safe to drop the three days example.

By striking out some examples from Table 1.4, Bill creates Table 1.8.

BILL   Hmm, for economy parking let's get rid of the three hours example as we already cover four hours.

TONY   And we should drop the three days example here as well.

BILL   Yes, you're right.

Bill again cuts from the economy parking examples to the ones in Table 1.9.

BILL   All right, for short-term we may cut down the examples by dropping one hour and thirty minutes, two hours, and twelve hours and thirty minutes.

TONY   Wait a minute, Bill. I think we shouldn't drop the twelve hours thirty minutes example. It reflects the daily maximum of $24.00.

BILL   Oh, you're right. Let's put that back in.

Table 1.8 Long-Term Garage
Parking Examples After Removing
Additional Examples

Parking Duration	Parking Costs
30 minutes	$2.00
1 hour	$2.00
3 hours	$6.00
6 hours	$12.00
7 hours	$12.00
24 hours	$12.00
1 day, 1 hour	$14.00
1 day, 3 hours	$18.00
1 day, 7 hours	$24.00
~~3 days~~	~~$36.00~~
6 days	$72.00
6 days, 1 hour	$72.00
7 days	$72.00
1 week, 1 days	$96.00
3 weeks	$216.00

Table 1.9 Economy Parking Examples
After Bill Removed Some Examples

Parking Duration	Parking Costs
30 minutes	$2.00
1 hour	$2.00
~~3 hours~~	~~$6.00~~
4 hours	$8.00
5 hours	$9.00
6 hours	$9.00
24 hours	$9.00
1 day, 1 hour	$11.00
1 day, 3 hours	$15.00
1 day, 5 hours	$18.00
~~3 days~~	~~$27.00~~
6 days	$54.00
6 days, 1 hour	$54.00
7 days	$54.00
1 week, 2 days	$72.00
3 weeks	$162.00

Table 1.10 Short-Term Parking Examples
After Removing Redundant Examples

Parking Duration	Parking Costs
30 minutes	$2.00
1 hour	$2.00
~~1 hour 30 minutes~~	~~$3.00~~
~~2 hours~~	~~$4.00~~
3 hours 30 minutes	$7.00
12 hours	$24.00
12 hours 30 minutes	$24.00
1 day 30 minutes	$25.00
1 day 1 hour	$26.00

Bill strikes out superfluous examples for short-term parking as visible in Table 1.10.

BILL   Finally, let's take a look on the valet parking examples. I don't see an example I would like to drop from these.

TONY   Agreed. These already represent the essentials of the business rules as you explained them to us.

PHYLLIS   OK, then we seem to have our scope for the stories on parking lots settled. Thanks, Bill and Tony.

Summary

In this chapter we saw how a collaborative meeting with business experts, programmers, and testers can settle and agree upon the requirements for the software. Although initially Tony could contribute only a few ideas, he helped to reach a common understanding by making the examples visible. With his unique testing knowledge, Tony could contribute to the discussion and focus the abstract discussion on concrete examples with the tables he created for the parking scenarios.

After Tony brought in the first table with examples, the group had a more meaningful discussion about the requirements. Phyllis the programmer recognized a bug in the examples they had identified for the economy parking lot. She asked for clarification about the case for six hours and one minute. Based on the examples the three had a conversation about the expected behavior from the business perspective.

Bill articulated his thoughts more meaningfully as well. He could directly see whether he agreed with the denoted examples. For the valet parking examples, even before seeing the first table that Tony created, Bill could directly tell how much the parking for twenty-four hours and one minute will cost. At the point where the first example was written down, the team communication in this Specification Workshop gained momentum.

During the discussion in the workshop, everyone was able to contribute. Phyllis threw in her perspective, while Tony brought in his critical thinking for edge cases. Phyllis spotted a bug in the economy examples before implementing a single line of code. The removal of that defect costs just a few words instead of going through the whole development cycle later.

Tony worked through the initial specification that Bill gave. He derived examples from the specification and explored corner conditions like twenty-four hours and one minute in order to get the correct answer from Bill right now. One of the questions would have been unanswered within the iteration. At the point where the team realized this flaw, Bill might have been on a business trip, unable to answer their demanding questions. At that point, the team could have gone with one interpretation for the implementation. If their interpretation is wrong at that point, the problem might become visible during the customer presentation, or even later when the product is in production for months.

Still, Bill, the business expert, made all the relevant decisions about the software, what to keep and what to throw out. When he mentioned that the costs for valet parking of twenty-four hours and one minute are $36.00, he said that the costs were obvious to him, still, Tony's question revealed an underlying assumption from Bill. Through the diversity of the participants the team could agree upon a common target for the implementation very easily.

The five cleaned-up tables that the team discussed are shown in Tables 1.11, 1.12, 1.13, 1.14, and 1.15. The team will implement and automate these soon. In

Table 1.11 Final Valet Parking Examples

Parking Duration	Parking Costs
30 minutes	$12.00
3 hours	$12.00
5 hours	$12.00
5 hours 1 minute	$18.00
12 hours	$18.00
24 hours	$18.00
1 day 1 minute	$36.00
3 days	$54.00
1 week	$126.00

Agile methods this might be the next iteration, or an iteration within the next three months. Since team members had a conversation about the requirements and manifested their understanding in essential examples, implementing the story with the agreed upon specification will be clear even at some later point in time.

Table 1.12 Final Short-Term Parking Examples

Parking Duration	Parking Costs
30 minutes	$2.00
1 hour	$2.00
3 hours 30 minutes	$7.00
12 hours	$24.00
12 hours 30 minutes	$24.00
1 day 30 minutes	$25.00
1 day 1 hour	$26.00

Table 1.13 Final Economy Parking Examples

Parking Duration	Parking Costs
30 minutes	$2.00
1 hour	$2.00
4 hours	$8.00
5 hours	$9.00
6 hours	$9.00
24 hours	$9.00
1 day, 1 hour	$11.00
1 day, 3 hours	$15.00
1 day, 5 hours	$18.00
6 days	$54.00
6 days, 1 hour	$54.00
7 days	$54.00
1 week, 2 days	$72.00
3 weeks	$162.00

Table 1.14 Final Long-Term Garage Parking Examples

Parking Duration	Parking Costs
30 minutes	$2.00
1 hour	$2.00
3 hours	$6.00
6 hours	$12.00
7 hours	$12.00
24 hours	$12.00
1 day, 1 hour	$14.00
1 day, 3 hours	$18.00
1 day, 7 hours	$24.00
6 days	$72.00
6 days, 1 hour	$72.00
7 days	$72.00
1 week, 2 days	$96.00
3 weeks	$216.00

Table 1.15 Final Long-Term Surface Parking Examples

Parking Duration	Parking Costs
30 minutes	$2.00
1 hour	$2.00
5 hours	$10.00
6 hours	$10.00
24 hours	$10.00
1 day, hour	$12.00
1 day, 3 hours	$16.00
1 day, 6 hours	$20.00
6 days	$60.00
6 days, 1 hour	$60.00
7 days	$60.00
1 week, 2 days	$80.00
3 weeks	$180.00

Chapter 2

Valet Parking Automation

The team decides to start with the Valet Parking examples from Table 1.11 of the parking lot story. The team chooses Cucumber[1] to automate the tests. Cucumber uses Ruby to glue together the data representation of the examples and the system under test. Each set of tests in Cucumber is called a feature. A feature goes into a text file on its own.

In order to automate a test in Cucumber, we need a combination of features that holds our data, some definition of test steps to interact with the application under test, as well as a set of environmental settings.

Tony has the diagram shown in Figure 2.1 in mind for the overall architecture.

The examples on the top are the ones the team identified at the workshop. Tony is now going to feed them to Cucumber. Cucumber will need some kind of

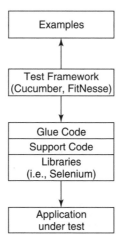

Figure 2.1 Test automation architecture that supports ATDD

1. http://cukes.info

glue code to exercise the application under test. The glue code can be split up into step definitions, support code, and third-party libraries like Selenium to drive the browser from the code.

Tony plans to grow a library of support code for the parking lot calculator. The glue code from the step definitions will use this library.

The automation setup will use Selenium.[2] Selenium drives a browser from the automation code. The automation code can then interact with webpages and check for correct values like the calculated parking costs. The team has set up a continuous integration system with a headless Selenium server[3] to which the tests will connect during the build.

The First Example

Tony picks the 30-minute examples first. He starts to describe the features for Valet Parking in the file `Valet.feature`. Tony writes his first test close to the table they ended up with in the workshop (see Listing 2.1).

Listing 2.1 Tony's first Valet Parking test

```
1 Feature: Valet Parking feature
2   The parking lot calculator calculates costs for Valet
      Parking.
3
4   Scenario: Calculate Valet Parking Cost for half an hour
5     When I park my car in the Valet Parking Lot for 30 minutes
6     Then I will have to pay $ 12.00
```

The Valet Parking feature includes thus far the first test for 30 minutes. The expected parking rate is $12.00 as discussed during the workshop. In Listing 2.1, the first line refers to the name of the feature that we're about to test. The second line describes this feature in prose terms. Cucumber displays this description on the console. Tony usually puts in anything into this description that communicates his intention to a future test author, also being aware that this might be himself in a few months time.

On line 4 he named his first test "Calculate Valet Parking Cost for half an hour." Since the first test just focuses on the parking duration of 30 minutes, he

---

2. http://seleniumhq.org

3. A headless Selenium server runs the browser on a virtual server. With a headless Selenium server you can run all of your tests on a machine without a monitor.

named it appropriately. The lines 5-6 use the keywords *When* and *Then* in order to express two distinct phases of one test.

The When-keyword describes any actions that should be taken in order to trigger the system under test to operate. This might include calling a function or pressing a button.

The name of the parking lot and the parking duration are in the When-keyword parameters. Cucumber will parse these and feed them into the system so that the application can calculate the parking costs.

The Then-keyword describes any post conditions of the test after it executed the application. Any desired effects of the application are put here. In the particular test Tony included a check for the calculated parking costs.

At this point Tony saves the file `Valet.feature` and runs it through Cucumber by issuing the command `cucumber Valet.feature`. Tony gets the output shown in Listing 2.2. It shows the first scenario that Tony just entered into his text editor. In line 8 it tells Tony that Cucumber tried to run one scenario, from which one was undefined. Cucumber identified also two undefined steps in line 9. Starting in line 12, Tony gets a hint on how to implement the missing steps.

Listing 2.2 Shell output from first Valet Parking test

```
1 Feature: Valet Parking feature
2   The parking lot calculator can calculate costs for Valet
      Parking.
3
4   Scenario: Calculate Valet Parking Cost
        # Valet.feature:4
5     When I park my car in the Valet Parking Lot for 30 minutes
        # Valet.feature:5
6     Then I will have to pay $ 12.00
        # Valet.feature:6
7
8 1 scenario (1 undefined)
9 2 steps (2 undefined)
10 0m0.001s
11
12 You can implement step definitions for undefined steps with
      these snippets:
13
```

```
14 When /^I park my car in the Valet Parking Lot for (\d+)
       minutes$/ do |arg1|
15    pending # express the regexp above with the code you wish
       you had
16 end
17
18 Then /^I will have to pay \$ (\d+)\.(\d+)$/ do |arg1, arg2|
19    pending # express the regexp above with the code you wish
       you had
20 end
21
22 If you want snippets in a different programming language, just
       make sure a file
23 with the appropriate file extension exists where cucumber
       looks for step definitions.
```

As prompted by Cucumber, Tony creates a file for the step definitions by copying and pasting the provided example from the shell output to a new file called `Valet_steps.rb`. In order to separate the test data from the glue code that exercises the instructions on the system under test, Tony puts the support code into a file in a new folder called `step_definitions`.

Tony makes some adaptions to the suggested method stubs. These adaptations will become handy later when he will extend the first example with different parking durations. The result is listed in Listing 2.3.

Cucumber can parse some variables from the textual examples. Tony used this for the duration and the price. `pending` is a keyword that Cucumber will recognize, and report back, that this test is currently pending and probably just evolving. When Tony re-executes the test with the step definitions now in place, he gets the output shown in Listing 2.4.

Listing 2.3 Initial step definitions for first test

```
1 When /^I park my car in the Valet Parking Lot for (.*)$/ do
       |duration|
2    pending
3 end
4
5 Then /^I will have to pay (.*)$/ do |price|
6    pending
7 end
```

Listing 2.4 Shell output from first Valet Parking test with step definitions in place

```
 1 Feature: Valet Parking feature
 2   The parking lot calculator can calculate costs for Valet
     Parking.
 3
 4   Scenario: Calculate Valet Parking Cost
        # Valet.feature:4
 5     When I park my car in the Valet Parking Lot for 30 minutes
        # step_definitions/Valet_steps.rb:1
 6       TODO (Cucumber::Pending)
 7       ./step_definitions/Valet_steps.rb:2:in '/^I park my car
     in the Valet Parking Lot for (.*)$/'
 8       Valet.feature:5:in 'When I park my car in the Valet
     Parking Lot for 30 minutes'
 9     Then I will have to pay $ 12.00
        # step_definitions/Valet_steps.rb:5
10
11 1 scenario (1 pending)
12 2 steps (1 skipped, 1 pending)
13 0m0.002s
```

In order to execute the system under test, Tony also needs to configure the
driver for the web browser, Selenium. Selenium comes with a server component
and a client library that his support code can use to drive the browser and navigate
on web pages. Tony writes this support code into its own file env.rb, so that
he can keep it separate from the glue code that exercises the system under test.
He places the file into a newly created subfolder etc (see the folder layout in
Figure 2.2). Everything he needs to have in place for that is listed in Listing 2.5.

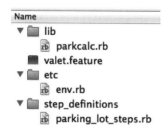

Figure 2.2 The folder layout after Tony put everything in place

Listing 2.5 Support code for setting up the Selenium client

```
1 require 'rubygems'
2 gem 'selenium-client'
3 require 'selenium/client'
4 require 'spec/expectations'
5 require 'lib/parkcalc'
6
7 # before all
8 selenium_driver = Selenium::Client::Driver.new \
9   :host => 'localhost',
10   :port => 4444,
11   :browser => '*firefox',
12   :url => 'http://www.shino.de/parkcalc',
13   :timeout_in_second => 60
14 selenium_driver.start_new_browser_session
15 $parkcalc = ParkCalcPage.new(selenium_driver)
16
17 # after all
18 at_exit do
19   selenium_driver.close_current_browser_session
20 end
```

This support code makes use of the Selenium library, starts a browser, and opens the ParkCalc page. When all the tests have executed, it will close the browser window again.

The file env.rb also requires a library for the parking lot calculator, lib/parkcalc. Tony will grow this library incrementally while developing his tests. The initial contents for this file are shown in Listing 2.6.

Listing 2.6 Initial ParkCalcPage class

```
1 class ParkCalcPage
2   attr :page
3
4   def initialize(page_handle)
5     @page = page_handle
6     @page.open '/parkcalc'
7   end
8 end
```

In the initializer the passed-in page_handle is stored into the local page attribute, and the /parkcalc page is opened. As a first implementation, this does the job of opening the web form using the browser that gets passed in from the setup in env.rb.

Tony starts to develop the first test step-wise. The first step he has to implement is the filling in of the parking duration parameters into the web interface. Tony does not yet know about the particular implementation details, but he has seen some hand-painted designs for the final layout. The When I park my car in the Valet Parking Lot for <duration> keyword has two basic steps. First, it needs to select the proper parking lot. Second, it has to fill in values to match the correct parking duration. Tony applies wishful thinking to this particular problem and writes down in Valet_steps.rb what he would like to have as an API in this particular case (see Listing 2.7).

Listing 2.7 Initial wishful implementation of the first keyword

```
1 When /^I park my car in the Valet Parking Lot for (.*)$/ do
    |duration|
2   $parkcalc.select('Valet Parking')
3   $parkcalc.enter_parking_duration(duration)
4   pending
5 end
```

The first part of the step is denoted on line 2 of Listing 2.7. Tony decided to have a selection mechanism for the parking lot. Depending on the implementation details, this might mean entering the given string into a text field, selecting the proper lot from a combo box, or picking the parking lot from a dropdown menu. Because Tony does not know anything about this yet, he postpones the implementation of this particular detail until the implementation of the ParkCalcPage class.

The second step on line 3 of Listing 2.7 describes that the parking duration is somehow filled in. Again, this might mean putting the text into a text field as is or having a parking start and end date time to calculate for this particular duration and filling it into two date fields. Because the implementation of the user interface is still open, Tony postpones the decision on how to implement the ParkCalcPage class.

In order to indicate that the test step definition is not complete, Tony leaves the pending keyword at the end of the keyword definition. The future implementor of the keyword will be reminded to edit the step definition once the other two keywords have been implemented.

Tony now informs the future implementor of the ParkCalcPage class about the interface decisions he has just made by providing empty implementations for his two expected methods (see Listing 2.8).

Listing 2.8 Empty implementations added to the ParkCalcPage class

```
1  class ParkCalcPage
2    attr :page
3
4    def initialize(page_handle)
5      @page = page_handle
6      @page.open '/parkcalc'
7    end
8
9    def select(parking_lot)
10   end
11
12   def enter_parking_duration(duration)
13   end
14
15 end
```

Tony adds the methods `select(parking_lot)` as well as `enter_parking_duration(duration)` to the ParkCalcPage. The first one will select the proper parking lot in the future. The second one is responsible for filling in whatever duration the user interface will offer.

Tony now focuses his attention on the verification step in the test he implemented. Similarly to the preparation steps, Tony applies wishful thinking in order to express the final verification of the parking costs. Listing 2.9 shows the changes he makes to `step_definitions/Valet_steps.rb`. The necessary changes to the ParkCalcPage class are shown in Listing 2.10.

Listing 2.9 Initial wishful implementation of the first keyword

```
1  Then /^I will have to pay (.*)$/ do |price|
2    $parkcalc.parking_costs.should == price
3    pending
4  end
```

Listing 2.10 Empty implementation of the parking cost calculation step

```
1   def parking_costs
2     return nil
3   end
```

Tony has now finished the first test as far as he can drive it. He is facing a decision on how to continue. On one hand, he can include the remaining examples from the workshop on Valet Parking. On the other hand, he can now also pair up with a developer to automate the examples in order to drive the development of the feature. A third alternative is to work on the remaining four parking lots and get the first test done in Cucumber. Tony decides to pair up with a developer to implement the first Valet Parking functionality and automate his first test. Tony can get the feedback from his work so far and continue to develop the tests later. Another advantage of this approach will be that Tony is not providing too many failing tests before the implementation starts.

Pairing for the First Test

Tony pairs up with Alex to implement and automate the first test. Alex already created a first layout for the website. Alex introduces Tony to his idea.

ALEX   Hi Tony, you're interested in seeing the parking cost calculator evolve?

TONY   Actually, I wanted to pair up with you in order to get the first test automated.

ALEX   Oh, wonderful. Which one did you start with?

TONY   Valet Parking. I introduced the first test for 30 minutes. I just checked in the first pending example before I came over.

ALEX   OK, let me show you what I've done so far.

Alex shows Tony the initial layout of the web page he designed (see Figure 2.3).

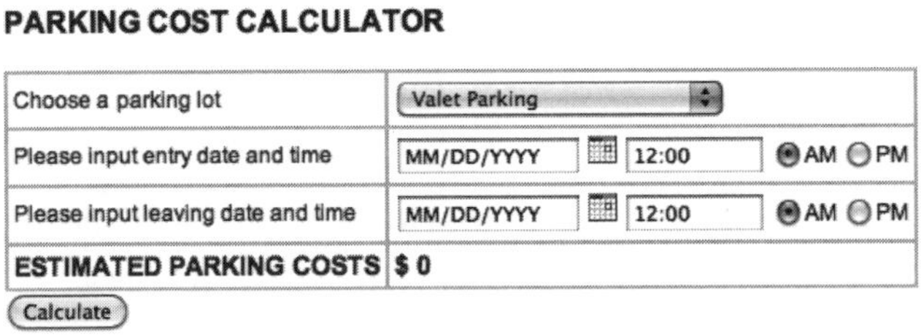

PARKING COST CALCULATOR

Choose a parking lot	Valet Parking		
Please input entry date and time	MM/DD/YYYY	12:00	● AM ○ PM
Please input leaving date and time	MM/DD/YYYY	12:00	● AM ○ PM
ESTIMATED PARKING COSTS	**$ 0**		

Calculate

Figure 2.3 Alex's mockup for the airline parking lot calculator

Initializers

ALEX   I designed the different parking lots as a dropdown box. The input date can be entered via a text field directly, or you can use the date picker in a calendar format. The time for the entry and leaving times are free text with a radio button to indicate AM or PM. The estimated parking costs will be shown when the Calculate button is pressed.

TONY   This looks good. Now, the following step definitions are pending, and we need to hook up to them now. Look at these.

ALEX   OK, this doesn't look too complicated. Let's start with the selection of the parking lot from the dropdown. I used the id "ParkingLot" here. So, selecting the proper value from the dropdown is a single step, like this.

Alex implements the `select` method in `lib/parkcalc.rb` as in Listing 2.11.

Listing 2.11 Selecting the right parking lot entry from the dropdowns

```
1    def select(parking_lot)
2      @page.select 'ParkingLot', parking_lot
3    end
```

TONY   OK, this seems intuitive. I select the passed-in parameter from the element with the id "ParkingLot." Nice. What about entering the parking duration?

ALEX   This may require a bit more thought. Let's use a hash in Ruby for this. In the future you can extend the value for entry and exit date and time then model all the different durations that you will need. If I remember the pieces I saw in the examples from the workshop correctly, there will be quite a few different values for this.

TONY   How do we do this?

ALEX   We will basically do a lookup from the duration string you pass into this function for the actual values for entry date, entry time, entry AM or PM, exit date, exit time, and exit AM or PM and pass them into the web page. These six values represent the six fields in the form I built. But let's define the hashmap first.

Alex creates a duration map at the top of the ParkCalcPage class (see Listing 2.12).

TONY   The two @'s there are indicating that durationMap is a class variable. Is this correct?

Listing 2.12 The map that holds durations and maps to actual dates and times

```
1   @@durationMap = {
2     '30 minutes' => ['05/04/2010', '12:00', 'AM', '05/04/2010'
      , '12:30', 'AM']
3   }
```

ALEX   Right. We will now use this hashmap to get the six values we are interested in. Let me show you how we will get the values out of the map.

Alex starts to implement the `enter_parking_duration` function (see Listing 2.13).

Listing 2.13 The six parameters for the form are derived from the durationMap

```
1   def enter_parking_duration(duration)
2     startingDate, startingTime, startingTimeAMPM, leavingDate,
      leavingTime, leavingTimeAMPM = @@durationMap[duration]
3   end
```

ALEX   Now, let's use these values and put them into the form. Let's start with the starting dates and times.

Alex extends the method that enters the parking duration with the changes in Listing 2.14.

Listing 2.14 The starting date and time is filled into the proper form fields

```
1   def enter_parking_duration(duration)
2     startingDate, startingTime, startingTimeAMPM, leavingDate,
      leavingTime, leavingTimeAMPM = @@durationMap[duration]
3     @page.type 'StartingDate', startingDate
4     @page.type 'StartingTime', startingTime
5     @page.click "//input[@name='StartingTimeAMPM' and @value
      ='%s']" % startingTimeAMPM
6   end
```

TONY   Can you explain this? I have trouble understanding the last line.

ALEX   Let me explain this in a bit more detail. First we get our six parameters out of the hashmap using the provided duration as a key. Then we fill in the starting date and time accordingly.

TONY   Yeah, that's intuitive to me. But what's that gibberish in the last line
        doing there?

ALEX   This is how I locate values of the radio buttons. It's an xpath entry, which
        expresses where the radio element is located and what its value is. It tells
        the driver to click on the input, whose name is "StartingTimeAMPM"
        and whose value matches the one provided.

TONY   I tend to put this at some other place. This looks too technical to me to
        be held in this otherwise more abstract method.

ALEX   I think you're correct, Tony. But let's write it down in our notes and
        finish this function first. Filling the end date and time is still missing. This
        is similar to the starting times. But let's see first if this thing works now.

Alex starts executing the test, and both Alex and Tony watch a browser window
pop up, opening the parking lot calculator page, filling in the values for the parking
lot and the starting date and time. In the end the browser is closed, and the result
is shown.

TONY   This looks good. Let's continue with the duration. We still need to fill in
        the end date and time.

ALEX   Sure, the code is similar to the one for the start date and time. Let's copy
        and paste the code from above and change the variables. We will clean
        this up after we know that it's working.

Alex extends the duration method to also fill out the end date and times (see
Listing 2.15).

Listing 2.15 The leaving date and time are added to the previous function.

```
1   def enter_parking_duration(duration)
2     startingDate, startingTime, startingTimeAMPM, leavingDate,
      leavingTime, leavingTimeAMPM = @@durationMap[duration]
3     @page.type 'StartingDate', startingDate
4     @page.type 'StartingTime', startingTime
5     @page.click "//input[@name='StartingTimeAMPM' and @value
      ='%s']" % startingTimeAMPM
6
7     @page.type 'LeavingDate', leavingDate
8     @page.type 'LeavingTime', leavingTime
```

```
9     @page.click "//input[@name='LeavingTimeAMPM' and @value='%
      s']" % leavingTimeAMPM
10   end
```

Tony and Alex run these steps and check that the leaving date and time are filled in correctly.

ALEX   All right, this works. Let's clean this up now. The two code blocks look rather similar. Let's put them into a method of their own.

Alex and Tony create a new method to fill in either starting or leaving date and times and replace the calls step by step. They verify that their first test still executes properly after each little change. They end up with the code shown in Listing 2.16.

Listing 2.16 Extracted method for filling in parking durations

```
1   def enter_parking_duration(duration)
2     startingDate, startingTime, startingTimeAMPM, leavingDate,
      leavingTime, leavingTimeAMPM = @@durationMap[duration]
3     fill_in_date_and_time_for 'Starting', startingDate,
      startingTime, startingTimeAMPM
4     fill_in_date_and_time_for 'Leaving', leavingDate,
      leavingTime, leavingTimeAMPM
5   end
6
7   def fill_in_date_and_time_for(formPrefix, date, time, ampm)
8     @page.type "%sDate" % formPrefix, date
9     @page.type "%sTime" % formPrefix, time
10    @page.click "//input[@name='%sTimeAMPM' and @value='%s']"
      % [ formPrefix, ampm ]
11  end
```

ALEX   Now, let's take a look at extracting those gibberish xpath entries.

TONY   Shall we declare a constant expression for these?

ALEX   That was exactly my idea. But I also want to put the other constant strings into a variable, so we can easily change these in the future. Let's extract one after the other. First let's get rid of the xpath. We need a name for that variable. What would you call this?

TONY   What about "amPMRadioButtonTemplate"?

ALEX   That's OK with me. Shall we then put the time and date strings into
         timeTemplate and dateTemplate?

TONY   That sounds good to me. Let's also put the prefixes into startingPrefix
         and leavingPrefix.

ALEX   Right, and I would like to put the lotIdentifier into its own constant as
         well.

TONY   This looks fine now.

Listing 2.17 shows the final version of the ParkCalcPage class after Alex and
Tony have extracted the constants. The initialization steps are complete at this
point.

Listing 2.17 The final version of the ParkCalcPage for the initialization steps

```
1  class ParkCalcPage
2
3    @@lotIdentifier = 'ParkingLot'
4    @@startingPrefix = 'Starting'
5    @@leavingPrefix = 'Leaving'
6    @@dateTemplate = "%sDate"
7    @@timeTemplate = "%sTime"
8    @@amPMRadioButtonTemplate = "//input[@name='%sTimeAMPM' and
       @value='%s']"
9
10   @@durationMap = {
11     '30 minutes' => ['05/04/2010', '12:00', 'AM', '05/04/2010'
       , '12:30', 'AM']
12   }
13
14   attr :page
15
16   def initialize(page_handle)
17     @page = page_handle
18     @page.open '/parkcalc'
19   end
20
21   def select(parking_lot)
22     @page.select @@lotIdentifier, parking_lot
23   end
```

```
24
25   def enter_parking_duration(duration)
26     startingDate, startingTime, startingTimeAMPM, leavingDate,
       leavingTime, leavingTimeAMPM = @@durationMap[duration]
27     fill_in_date_and_time_for @@startingPrefix, startingDate,
       startingTime, startingTimeAMPM
28     fill_in_date_and_time_for @@leavingPrefix, leavingDate,
       leavingTime, leavingTimeAMPM
29   end
30
31   def fill_in_date_and_time_for(formPrefix, date, time, ampm)
32     @page.type @@dateTemplate % formPrefix, date
33     @page.type @@timeTemplate % formPrefix, time
34     @page.click @@amPMRadioButtonTemplate % [ formPrefix,
       ampm ]
35   end
36
37 end
```

Checking the Results

TONY   Now, let's check the output. We still didn't click the Calculate button that you put into the form, and we need to find a way to collect the calculated costs from the page.

ALEX   Sure. Let's start with taking out the pending statement from the step definition, so that our Then definition gets executed.

TONY   Oh, I would have forgotten that. That one could have cost me half a day to search for.

ALEX   Well, this is why we pair, isn't it?

TONY   While we're at it, we can take out the pending step from the check that we will be implementing in a few.

ALEX   Yes, right. Now, let's see how to check for the proper price. First, we need to click the calculate button. I want to add this to the parking_costs function as a first step before returning the costs. After that we need to wait for the page to load with the new results. Then we get the element holding the cost element and simply return it.

Alex implements the parking_costs function as in Listing 2.18.

Listing 2.18 The initial version of the check

```
1 def parking_costs
2   @page.click 'Submit'
3   @page.wait_for_page_to_load 10000
4   cost_element = @page.get_text "//tr[td/div[@class='SubHead']
      = 'estimated Parking costs']/td/span/b"
5   return cost_element
6 end
```

TONY   What does the constant 10000 mean there?

ALEX   It's a timeout value. The driver will wait for 10 seconds until either a new
        page loads successfully, or the test will fail.

TONY   Now, let's clean this gibberish up again. I propose to extract the xpath
        into a constant again.

ALEX   First, let's see if it already executes correctly. Let's start the test.

Alex and Tony begin the test, and watch it execute the parking lot calculator,
turning the console output in the end green, indicating that everything went well
(see Listing 2.19).

Listing 2.19 Shell output from first Valet Parking test

```
1 Feature: Valet Parking feature
2   The parking lot calculator can calculate costs for Valet
      Parking.
3
4   Scenario: Calculate Valet Parking Cost
        # Valet.feature:4
5   When I park my car in the Valet Parking Lot for 30 minutes
        # step_definitions/Valet_steps.rb:1
6   Then I will have to pay $ 12.00
        # step_definitions/Valet_steps.rb:6
7
8 1 scenario (1 passed)
9 2 steps (2 passed)
10 0m0.324s
```

TONY   All right, the test passes. Before we break anything, let's check this thing in, so that we can roll back any changes we make later. Just in case.

ALEX   Good idea.

Alex and Tony check everything they have so far into the version control system.

ALEX   Now back to your proposal. Good idea, but I would like to divide the function up into the two steps first. The first function is to click the Submit button and wait for the page to load. The second function will fetch the calculated costs and simply return them. Let me show you what I mean.

Alex extracts two methods from the initial `parking_costs` function (see Listing 2.20).

Listing 2.20 The check after factoring out two functions for the individual steps

```
1    def parking_costs
2      calculate_parking_costs
3      get_parking_costs_from_page
4    end
5
6    def calculate_parking_costs
7      @page.click 'Submit'
8      @page.wait_for_page_to_load 10000
9    end
10
11   def get_parking_costs_from_page
12     @page.get_text "//tr[td/div[@class='SubHead'] = 'estimated
         Parking costs']/td/span/b"
13   end
```

TONY   Now, let's put the xpath entry describing the location of the cost element into a constant.

ALEX   And while we're at it, let's put the name of the Calculate button into a meaningful variable as well.

TONY   Now, a final test run, and we are ready to check in our results into the source code repository.

Tony and Alex watch the test execute. It still passes. They check in the files into the source repository. Listing 2.21 shows the final text of step_definitions/valet_steps.rb and Listing 2.22 shows the final code for lib/parkcalc.rb.

Listing 2.21 The final version of the Valet Parking steps for the first test

```
1 When /^I park my car in the Valet Parking Lot for (.*)$/ do
      |duration|
2   $parkcalc.select('Valet Parking')
3   $parkcalc.enter_parking_duration(duration)
4 end
5
6 Then /^I will have to pay (.*)$/ do |price|
7   $parkcalc.parking_costs.should == price
8 end
```

Listing 2.22 The final version of the ParkCalcPage class for the first test

```
1 class ParkCalcPage
2
3   @@lotIdentifier = 'ParkingLot'
4   @@startingPrefix = 'Starting'
5   @@leavingPrefix = 'Leaving'
6   @@dateTemplate = "%sDate"
7   @@timeTemplate = "%sTime"
8   @@amPMRadioButtonTemplate = "//input[@name='%sTimeAMPM' and
      @value='%s']"
9
10  @@calculateButtonIdentifier = 'Submit'
11  @@costElementLocation = "//tr[td/div[@class='SubHead']
      = 'estimated Parking costs']/td/span/b"
12
13  @@durationMap = {
14    '30 minutes' => ['05/04/2010', '12:00', 'AM', '05/04/2010'
      , '12:30', 'AM']
15  }
16
17  attr :page
18
19  def initialize(page_handle)
```

```
20   @page = page_handle
21   @page.open '/parkcalc'
22  end
23
24  def select(parking_lot)
25   @page.select @@lotIdentifier, parking_lot
26  end
27
28  def enter_parking_duration(duration)
29   startingDate, startingTime, startingTimeAMPM, leavingDate,
       leavingTime, leavingTimeAMPM = @@durationMap[duration]
30   fill_in_date_and_time_for @@startingPrefix, startingDate,
       startingTime, startingTimeAMPM
31   fill_in_date_and_time_for @@leavingPrefix, leavingDate,
       leavingTime, leavingTimeAMPM
32  end
33
34  def fill_in_date_and_time_for(formPrefix, date, time, ampm)
35   @page.type @@dateTemplate % formPrefix, date
36   @page.type @@timeTemplate % formPrefix, time
37   @page.click @@amPMRadioButtonTemplate % [ formPrefix,
       ampm ]
38  end
39
40  def parking_costs
41   calculate_parking_costs
42   get_parking_costs_from_page
43  end
44
45  def calculate_parking_costs
46   @page.click @@calculateButtonIdentifier
47   @page.wait_for_page_to_load 10000
48  end
49
50  def get_parking_costs_from_page
51   @page.get_text @@costElementLocation
52  end
53 end
```

Tabulated Tests

Now, with the first example automated, Tony can easily reuse the steps he created for the first test in order to automate the remaining examples from the workshop. As a first step, he denotes the scenario from `Valet.feature` as a scenario outline with examples in a tabulated way. In order to get there, he replaces the duration of 30 minutes with a placeholder, `<parking duration>`, he replaces the expected price with the placeholder `<parking costs>`, and marks the scenario as a scenario outline. Tony puts the concrete values in a table holding all the examples below the scenario outline. Tony labels the columns with the names of the placeholders. This results in Listing 2.23.

Listing 2.23 The first test converted to a tabulated format

```
1 Feature: Valet Parking feature
2   The parking lot calculator can calculate costs for Valet
      Parking.
3
4   Scenario Outline: Calculate Valet Parking Cost
5     When I park my car in the Valet Parking Lot for <parking
        duration>
6     Then I will have to pay <parking costs>
7
8   Examples:
9   | parking duration | parking costs |
10  | 30 minutes       | $ 12.00       |
```

At this point, Tony has started to convert the workshop examples literally to a tabulated format. Tony executes the test to verify that it is still working properly. He gets the output shown in Listing 2.24.

Listing 2.24 Shell output with the first test in a tabulated format

```
1 Feature: Valet Parking feature
2   The parking lot calculator can calculate costs for Valet
      Parking.
3
4   Scenario Outline: Calculate Valet Parking Cost
                # Valet.feature:4
5     When I park my car in the Valet Parking Lot for <parking
        duration> # step_definitions/Valet_steps.rb:1
```

```
 6      Then I will have to pay <parking costs>
                  # step_definitions/Valet_steps.rb:6
 7
 8      Examples:
 9        | parking duration | parking costs |
10        | 30 minutes       | $ 12.00       |
11
12  1 scenario (1 passed)
13  2 steps (2 passed)
14  0m0.316s
```

Now he starts to fill in the remaining examples from the workshop. In the end Tony has put all the examples from the workshop into the tabulated test (see Listing 2.25).

Listing 2.25 All examples from the workshop filled into the table

```
 1 Feature: Valet Parking feature
 2   The parking lot calculator can calculate costs for Valet
     Parking.
 3
 4   Scenario Outline: Calculate Valet Parking Cost
 5     When I park my car in the Valet Parking Lot for <parking
       duration>
 6     Then I will have to pay <parking costs>
 7
 8     Examples:
 9     | parking duration | parking costs |
10     | 30 minutes       | $ 12.00       |
11     | 3 hours          | $ 12.00       |
12     | 5 hours          | $ 12.00       |
13     | 5 hours 1 minute | $ 18.00       |
14     | 12 hours         | $ 18.00       |
15     | 24 hours         | $ 18.00       |
16     | 1 day 1 minute   | $ 36.00       |
17     | 3 days           | $ 54.00       |
18     | 1 week           | $ 126.00      |
```

In order to execute all these tests, he has to extend the durationMap in the ParkCalcPage class with proper values (see Listing 2.26).

Listing 2.26 The ParkCalcPage class with the extended durationMap for all Valet Parking
                  tests

```
 1  class ParkCalcPage
 2
 3  ...
 4
 5    @@durationMap = {
 6      '30 minutes' => ['05/04/2010', '12:00', 'AM', '05/04/2010'
                         ,'12:30', 'AM'],
 7      '3 hours' => ['05/04/2010', '12:00', 'AM', '05/04/2010',
                      '03:00', 'AM'],
 8      '5 hours' => ['05/04/2010', '12:00', 'AM', '05/04/2010',
                      '05:00', 'AM'],
 9      '5 hours 1 minute' => ['05/04/2010', '12:00', 'AM',
                      '05/04/2010', '05:01', 'AM'],
10      '12 hours' => ['05/04/2010', '12:00', 'AM', '05/04/2010',
                      '12:00', 'PM'],
11      '24 hours' => ['05/04/2010', '12:00', 'AM', '05/05/2010',
                      '12:00', 'AM'],
12      '1 day 1 minute' => ['05/04/2010', '12:00', 'AM',
                      '05/05/2010', '12:01', 'AM'],
13      '3 days' => ['05/04/2010', '12:00', 'AM', '05/07/2010',
                      '12:00', 'AM'],
14      '1 week' => ['05/04/2010', '12:00', 'AM', '05/11/2010',
                      '12:00', 'AM']
15    }
16
17  ...
```

Tony executes all the tests and sees that they all pass. Alex seems to have
implemented the functionality for the Valet Parking lot completely. The acceptance
criteria on the back of the story card already provided Alex with the right answers
for the implementation. As a final step, Tony checks in all the files he touched
into the source code repository and indicates on the story for Valet Parking on the
team's taskboard that this story is automated and passing. Alex and Tony celebrate
this success with a high-five at the end of the day.

Summary

This concludes the automation for the Valet Parking examples. We saw that Tony started out with Cucumber. He wrote down the first example in a natural language into a text file. He then started to automate this first example up to the point he felt comfortable with at his level of expertise. When Tony got stuck with the automation code, he paired up with Alex, the test automation programmer.

Alex and Tony implemented the ParkCalcPage driver, which fills in the parking lot and the starting and leaving dates and times into the web page form. After clicking the Calculate button, the parking costs are returned from a function, so that the test framework is able to check the actual value against the expected one.

When Alex and Tony started to pair, they could both contribute from their unique expertise. Tony, the tester, could critically think about the test code while Alex the automation programmer could help Tony get over the technical burden of test automation. By working together, they helped each other see things from a different perspective as well. Finally, the code that Alex and Tony produced is reviewed by definition. Having a second pair of eyes looking over the code while it is created is extremely valuable in team-based software development—and that includes team-based test automation as well.

By converting the first test into a scenario outline, Tony was able to automate the remaining examples for Valet Parking from the workshop as directly as possible. The business expert, Bill, should be able to find the examples Phyllis, Tony, and he discussed during the workshop in the output of the tests.

Chapter 3

Automating the Remaining Parking Lots

As Tony finished the first tests for the Valet Parking lot, he was rather confident that he could automate the remaining four parking lot examples one by one in a few hours. Therefore he continued to do so directly, starting with the examples for the Short-Term Parking lot, then the Economy lot, the Long-Term Garage parking lot, and finally automating the Long-Term Surface Parking lot examples.

Short-Term Parking Lot

The Short-Term Parking lot examples from the end of the workshop are displayed in Table 3.1.

Table 3.1 Short-Term Parking Lot Examples

Parking Duration	Parking Costs
30 minutes	$2.00
1 hour	$2.00
3 hours 30 minutes	$7.00
12 hours	$24.00
12 hours 30 minutes	$24.00
1 day 30 minutes	$25.00
1 day 1 hour	$26.00

Tony starts automating these by using the Valet Parking examples as a basis. He creates `Short-Term.feature` with the contents listed in Listing 3.1.

Listing 3.1 The Short-Term Parking lot automated examples

```
1 Feature: Short-Term Parking feature
2   The parking lot calculator can calculate costs for
      Short-Term Parking.
```

```
3
4   Scenario Outline: Calculate Short-Term Parking Cost
5     When I park my car in the Short-Term Parking Lot for
      <parking duration>
6     Then I will have to pay <parking costs>
7
8   Examples:
9   | parking duration    | parking costs |
10  | 30 minutes          | $ 2.00        |
11  | 1 hour              | $ 2.00        |
12  | 1 hour 30 minutes   | $ 3.00        |
13  | 2 hours             | $ 4.00        |
14  | 3 hours 30 minutes  | $ 7.00        |
15  | 12 hours 30 minutes | $ 24.00       |
16  | 1 day 30 minutes    | $ 25.00       |
17  | 1 day 1 hour        | $ 26.00       |
```

Line 5 does not work immediately. None of the current step definitions match the "Short-Term Parking" part. Tony therefore inspects the step definitions from earlier. He realizes that he can reuse the step definitions nearly completely by just introducing a new pattern match for the parking lot used. First of all he renames step_definitions/valet_steps.rb to step_definitions/parking_lot _steps.rb and introduces the parking lot parameter in the when keyword definition. The result is listed in Listing 3.2.

Listing 3.2 The step definitions after Tony generalized them

```
1 When /^I park my car in the (.*) Lot for (.*)$/ do |
     parking_lot, duration|
2   $parkcalc.select(parking_lot)
3   $parkcalc.enter_parking_duration(duration)
4 end
5
6 Then /^I will have to pay (.*)$/ do |price|
7   $parkcalc.parking_costs.should == price
8 end
```

The final step for Tony for the Short-Term Parking tests is to extend the durationMap in the ParkCalcPage class. For the Short-Term Parking examples he needs to introduce examples for 1 hour, 1 hour 30 minutes, 2 hours, 3 hours 30 minutes, 12 hours 30 minutes, 1 day 30 minutes, and 1 day 1 hour. The resulting durationMap from lib/parkcalc.rb can be seen in Listing 3.3.

Listing 3.3 The ParkCalcPage class with the extended durationMap for all Valet and Short-Term Parking examples

```
1  class ParkCalcPage
2
3  ...
4    @@durationMap = {
5      '30 minutes' => ['05/04/2010', '12:00', 'AM', '05/04/2010'
                        , '12:30', 'AM'],
6      '1 hour' => ['05/04/2010', '12:00', 'AM', '05/04/2010',
                   '01:00', 'AM'],
7      '1 hour 30 minutes' => ['05/04/2010', '12:00', 'AM',
                   '05/04/2010', '01:30', 'AM'],
8      '2 hours' => ['05/04/2010', '12:00', 'AM', '05/04/2010',
                   '02:00', 'AM'],
9      '3 hours' => ['05/04/2010', '12:00', 'AM', '05/04/2010',
                   '03:00', 'AM'],
10     '3 hours 30 minutes' => ['05/04/2010', '12:00', 'AM',
                   '05/04/2010', '03:30', 'AM'],
11     '5 hours' => ['05/04/2010', '12:00', 'AM', '05/04/2010',
                   '05:00', 'AM'],
12     '5 hours 1 minute' => ['05/04/2010', '12:00', 'AM',
                   '05/04/2010', '05:01', 'AM'],
13     '12 hours' => ['05/04/2010', '12:00', 'AM', '05/04/2010',
                   '12:00', 'PM'],
14     '12 hours 30 minutes' => ['05/04/2010', '12:00', 'AM',
                   '05/04/2010', '12:30', 'PM'],
15     '24 hours' => ['05/04/2010', '12:00', 'AM', '05/05/2010',
                   '12:00', 'AM'],
16     '1 day 1 minute' => ['05/04/2010', '12:00', 'AM',
                   '05/05/2010', '12:01', 'AM'],
17     '1 day 30 minutes' => ['05/04/2010', '12:00', 'AM',
                   '05/05/2010', '12:30', 'AM'],
18     '1 day 1 hour' => ['05/04/2010', '12:00', 'AM',
                   '05/05/2010', '01:00', 'AM'],
```

```
19    '3 days' => ['05/04/2010', '12:00', 'AM', '05/07/2010',
         '12:00', 'AM'],
20    '1 week' => ['05/04/2010', '12:00', 'AM', '05/11/2010',
         '12:00', 'AM']
21  }
22  ...
```

Tony executes all the Short-Term Parking examples, and as he sees that they all pass, then he executes the whole suite with the Valet Parking as well as the Short-Term Parking examples again. He executes both because he is not sure whether the two test suites might interact with each other. As Tony sees both of them pass, he feels safe checking in his code to the version control system. Tony congratulates himself because he saved the company a lot of money by reusing the already existing automation code rather than re-inventing the wheel.

Economy Parking Lot

Tony takes a look at the Economy Parking examples next. The results from the workshop are listed in Table 3.2.

Tony creates the file `Economy.feature` where he describes the Economy Parking lot feature. The contents are listed in Listing 3.4.

Table 3.2 Economy Parking Lot Examples

Parking Duration	Parking Costs
30 minutes	$2.00
1 hour	$2.00
4 hours	$8.00
5 hours	$9.00
6 hours	$9.00
24 hours	$9.00
1 day, 1 hour	$11.00
1 day, 3 hours	$15.00
1 day, 5 hours	$18.00
6 days	$54.00
6 days, 1 hour	$54.00
7 days	$54.00
1 week, 2 days	$72.00
3 weeks	$162.00

Listing 3.4 The Economy Parking Lot automated examples

```
 1 Feature: Economy Parking feature
 2   The parking lot calculator can calculate costs for Economy
       parking.
 3
 4   Scenario Outline: Calculate Economy Parking Cost
 5     When I park my car in the Economy Parking Lot for <parking
         duration>
 6     Then I will have to pay <parking costs>
 7
 8   Examples:
 9   | parking duration    | parking costs |
10   | 30 minutes          | $ 2.00        |
11   | 1 hour              | $ 2.00        |
12   | 4 hours             | $ 8.00        |
13   | 5 hours             | $ 9.00        |
14   | 6 hours             | $ 9.00        |
15   | 24 hours            | $ 9.00        |
16   | 1 day, 1 hour       | $ 11.00       |
17   | 1 day, 3 hours      | $ 15.00       |
18   | 1 day, 5 hours      | $ 18.00       |
19   | 6 days              | $ 54.00       |
20   | 6 days, 1 hour      | $ 54.00       |
21   | 7 days              | $ 54.00       |
22   | 1 week, 2 days      | $ 72.00       |
23   | 3 weeks             | $ 162.00      |
```

As a last step, Tony extends the durationMap in the ParkCalcPage class to include the new values. I will leave this extension to the ambitious reader as an exercise. Before checking the Economy examples in the version control system, Tony executes all tests again.

Tony repeats the cycle for the two variations of the Long-Term Parking lot. I will leave this as an exercise for the enthusiastic reader. You can find the full examples on the github repository for this part of the book.[1]

---

1. http://github.com/mgaertne/airport

Summary

Tony was able to automate the remaining examples quickly. Since Alex and Tony worked in a modular way, automating the remaining four parking lots was easy to do—even for Tony, who is a rather inexperienced programmer. The resulting automated tests describe the specification of the parking cost calculator as agreed upon with the customer. The examples are automated, and can be used for future adaptions of the underlying logic.

Tony also noticed that he could reuse most of the automation code that was available from the Valet Parking examples. Rather than coming up with a different approach here, he simply extended the lookup map for the different parking durations, varied the picking of the parking lot, and then noted the examples.

Chapter 4

Wish and Collaborate

After this short iteration we will take a step back and reflect briefly. The functionality of the airport parking lot calculator was developed. Before the iteration started, the team discussed the requirements for the application that they should build. The format they used was a specification workshop [Adz09, Adz11]. The team identified different parking lots, and in that conversation they noted examples for different parking durations and the costs respectively.

After the examples were clear to the team, they started to work on the functionality. This particular team seems to work in parallel on coding and testing tasks. The tester wrote down the first example for the automation. After that he worked his way through the framework until he got stuck with the automation. You may recall that Tony started with a happy path example. When automating your examples, this is essential because it forces you to get the implementation correct right from the start before fiddling with too many details and corner conditions. The first example will provide insights about the necessary user interface for the end user. Starting from this basis, you can extend the examples in multiple directions. It does not really matter which happy path example you start with, if you apply responsive design techniques and object-oriented design. In this example there wasn't much magic happening to the automation code, but there are some possible evolution points for this code. For one example all the dates seem to cluster around one particular date. In a future version of the automation code you may want to vary this, maybe leaving the calculation of particular durations to a helper class like a DurationFactory, which calculates randomized starting dates.

One important thing happened when Tony got up and walked over to a programmer, maybe the most important thing about successful test automation. A tester and a programmer collaborating in order to achieve the team goal of test automation provides great value when introducing the ATDD approach. Despite leaving Tony alone with the task to automate the tests, Alex offers him full support for the first test. Tony learned from Alex some of the underlying design principles and how to treat code to keep it readable and maintainable. Over time Tony got more and more familiar with test automation code. This enabled him to proceed with the automation code.

Let's take a look at each of the three elements we saw here: specification workshops, wishful thinking, and collaboration.

Specification Workshops

In specification workshops teams discuss the stories for upcoming iterations. At first specification workshops appeared to me as a waterfall approach to requirements. Programmers and testers get together with some business representative to nail down requirements. But there are more benefits for agile teams to hold these workshops.

Getting everyone involved helps build a common language for the project. Eric Evans calls this language the ubiquitous language [Eva03]. When programmers, testers, and business people get their heads together to reach a common understanding about the project, they can sort out many misunderstandings before these blow up the whole project.

A workshop can help the whole team reach that shared understanding. There are some things you will have to keep in mind in order to make these workshops a success for everyone–regardless of whether they may be participating.

First of all, you should not waste the time of your business representatives. If you invite an expert user to your specification workshop, everyone in the room should respect the precious time of this person. A business representative could be a ProductOwner, a real user, or a subject matter expert for the application domain. If your team starts to discuss the latest technology at such a workshop, the business representative is probably going to reject your invitation the next time. At that point you will have lost crucial information for your application.

Pre-select some stories from your backlog. If you know which stories you will most likely implement in the near future, you can sort them out. If you end up with a list of stories that is probably too large to discuss in your allotted time for the workshop, then you have to cut it further.

For stories where the business flow seems obvious or straightforward to you, you can prepare data and bring those to the workshop. The business representative will value your engagement in the project and the easier stories. By preparing examples, you will also help keep the businessperson engaged and seeing the advantages of these workshops.

During the workshop it is crucial to ask clarifying questions. You can prepare yourself by going through the stories with your team and collecting open questions for the moment. Over time you may gain experience to come up more spontaneously with clarifying questions, but initially you may need full team feedback for the stories.

Finally, one element I consider mandatory for any meeting or workshop is visualization. Rather than leaving the discussion abstract, note down what you understand and ask for agreement based on your notes. You can do this publicly on a flipchart, or take notes on paper and share them around the table. For larger meetings I prefer flipcharts, while in a setting of three participants as in this first example, a piece of paper will suffice.

If your customer is located in a completely different country or timezone, you may want to try a different multimedia setting. With instant messaging and screen-sharing tools around, you can easily collaborate even if you are not in the same room with the whole team. However, you should set some preparation time aside to get these tools set up before the meeting.

Wishful Thinking

A vital implementation of acceptance test-driven development includes at least two spoonfuls of wishful thinking. In the example at the Major International Airport Corp. we saw Tony implementing the tests without any previous knowledge about details of the parking cost calculator.

Instead, Tony applied wishful thinking in order to automate the examples that the team had identified in the workshop. Tony avoided considering the available user interface. Instead, he used the interface he wished he would have. The examples clearly stated that there are different durations to be considered for different parking costs. The entry and exit dates did not play a role when writing down the examples with the business expert. Tony didn't clutter up his examples with these unnecessary details.

Instead of programming against a real user interface, abstract from the GUI to the business cases behind your examples. As Tony demonstrated, consider that you could have any interface for your tests. Dale Emery recommended writing your tests as if you already have the interface you wish you had. Use the most readable interface to automate your examples. If you hook your automation code to the application under test, you may find out that you have to write a lot of code to get the application automated. If you listen to your tests [FP09], you will find that your application needs a different interface—at least for your automated tests.

Wishful thinking is especially powerful if you can apply it before any code is written. At the time you start implementing your production code, you can discover the interface your application needs in order to be testable. In our example, we saw that Tony and Alex started their work in parallel. The interface that Alex designed is sufficient for the discussed examples, but the lack of input parking durations directly forces the need for more test automation code.

The translation between parking durations and entry and exit dates and times is simple in this example. You may have noticed that all the examples start on the same date. Most testers and programmers faced with these hard-coded values feel uneasy about it. While it takes little effort to generate parking duration on the fly while the tests execute, the amount and complexity of support code would rise. As a software developer, I would love to write unit tests for this complex code and drive the implementation of the support code using test-driven development.

The translation between durations, entry and exit dates and times is an early sign that something might be wrong. Maybe the user interface is wrong. But as a customer at an airport, I would probably like to input my departure and arrival dates and times. So, the user interface seems to be correct based on the goal of the potential customers.

Another option could be that the tests point to a missing separation of concerns. Currently, the calculator calculates the parking duration first, and after that the parking costs. The cost calculation could be extracted from the code, so that it becomes testable separately without the need to drive the examples through the user interface.

In the end, your tests make suggestions for your interface design. This applies to unit tests as well as acceptance tests. When testers and programmers work in isolation, a more problematic interface for test automation can manifest itself than when both programmers and testers work together on that problem.

Collaboration

In the story of the Major International Airport Corp. we saw collaboration on multiple levels. Tony, the tester, joined the workshop together with Bill, the business expert, and Phyllis, the programmer. Later, while automating the examples they had identified in the workshop, Tony worked together with Alex.

Collaboration is another key ingredient to a successful ATDD approach. Consider what would happen if Tony worked out the examples by himself. He probably could have caught many problems within the software. These defects would have been bounced back and forth between Tony and the programmers— eventually getting both upset. In the end, when the product finally was delivered, the customer would have been unhappy about the misinterpreted corner conditions.

If this sounds familiar to you, consider a project that starts with a workshop. In this workshop most ambiguities would be settled between the programmers and the testers. The remaining questions would get answered before the team starts to work on the implementation. Since the examples express the requirements for the software, the team knows exactly when it has finished the implementation. There is some back and forth between testers and programmers. The programmers eventually find out about the value the automated examples bring them if they execute them before checking in their code to the version control system. In the end, the project delivers on time and with no problems.

To most teams new to acceptance test-driven development this may sound like a fairy tale. But there are many success stories of successful software delivery using an approach like ATDD in combination with other agile practices like refactoring, test-driven development (TDD), continuous integration, and the whole team approach. The combination of technical excellence on one hand and teamwork on the other hand seems to be a magic ingredient.

I also apply collaboration when automating tests. After all, test automation is software development and therefore, I want to apply all the practices and techniques that I also apply to production code. Most of the time I even take more care implementing support code for my tests than I take care for the production code. This means that I apply test-driven development, refactoring, and continuous integration to the support code as well.

Tony worked with Cucumber before he could get started with the support code. But he clearly did not have the expertise to finish the test automation code all on his own. When he noticed that he was stuck, he stopped work, and approached that team member that could help him and had the expertise with programming. Most teams new to ATDD confuse the collaboration aspect with the need for every tester to code. It makes the life of testers easier if they can work independently from programmers on tests and test automation, though. That's why over time testers start to learn more and more tricks to automate their tests, but this is not a precondition. It is rather an outcome and a side effect in the long term.

Once I taught the approach to testers at a medical supplier. The testers were former nurses and had no technical education at all. Up to that point they tested the application manually. The programmers pushed forward for more test automation, but lacked the domain expertise the testers had. They agreed on an approach where the testers would get started with the examples, and the programmers would write most of the support code to get the examples automated.

Lack of programming knowledge does not mean that you cannot get started with the approach. Besides pen and paper, Tony didn't need anything at all to get the examples down and use them as a communication device. In fact, most teams should start with such an approach, not automating the examples at all. The enhanced communication already improves the development process. You won't get the full benefits of applying the whole approach, but the improved communication and collaboration will get you started. This comes in handy especially if you deal with a legacy code base that is not (yet) prepared to deal with automation code.

Summary

Specification workshops, wishful thinking, and collaboration add so much to your overall testing concert. First, to make sure that your team builds the right thing, you talk to your customer. By working closely together on the acceptance criteria you form a ubiquitous understanding in your team.

Starting from the business user goals, you apply wishful thinking to form the API that you wished your application had. You build your automated tests then against this API that will support all the testability functions that you will need. Your application becomes testable with automated tests by definition and at the same time you make sure that your tests don't get too coupled to the actual implementation of the user interface.

Finally, a thing we all need to remember from time to time is we are not alone in software development. That means that we may work together with others for support when our work gets tough. This especially holds true when you work on a team that is new to agile development and consists of many specialists. In order to perform on a higher level, you will need to work with your teammates to learn some of their special skills. Over time you will be able to compensate for vacation times and sick leaves if you can replace each other.

Part II

Traffic Light Software System

Specification workshops, wishful thinking, and collaboration might serve you well in the beginning. But you can extend the ATDD approach even more. A multitude of teams have experimented with very different solutions to the problems they were facing after applying ATDD for a while. A collection of these solutions can be found in *Specification by Example* [Adz11].

Rather than showing a solution from one team here, I would like to challenge the constraints that some teams imposed on themselves while applying ATDD. The "driven" part of the name suggests that it is possible to drive the application code from the examples. With a combination of lessons I learned from test-driven development, and what I found myself doing at times, in this part I will pair up with you, dear reader, in order to work through a system using ATDD and TDD while the design of the domain code grows.

In this part we will take a look at a traffic light control system. We will evolve a system together over the course of the development. Similarly, we will evolve the tests together with the system. At times we will examine portions of the support code to gain insights into possible designs for the production code. The tests will be automated based on an API in Java using FitNesse with SLiM.

Since I plan to pair up with you, we will leave the narrative style I used in Part II. We will work through the examples together, but we should start with a specification workshop first. Since I am from Germany, and Germany has quite different traffic light rules compared to other countries in the world, we have to get to a common understanding of the application domain first. Let's get started with this.

Chapter 5
Getting Started

In this chapter we will take a closer look at some of the prerequisites. Traffic lights are handled differently in different countries. Therefore, I will introduce some of the requirements to you first.

In this part we will be dealing with a second test framework, FitNesse, so I will provide a very brief introduction. If you want to dive deeper later, take a look at Appendix B for a more in-depth introduction.

FitNesse comes with another programming language to write the glue and support code in. We will also work on the production code in this part. Don't be scared now. That is why we pair. I will provide you a brief introduction to the programming language in order to get you started.

We will also see how ATDD is supplemented with TDD. We will start with a test for the business functionality. After that, we will deal with a developer focus on classes and how to drive the design of the underlying source code. In fact, we use the acceptance tests as an approach to explore the domain, so that we can start writing production classes with a better understanding about the application domain and the resulting model.

Traffic Lights

In most larger cities I have visited, traffic lights for pedestrians are rather suggestions than part of the traffic rule system. While researching laws for traffic light systems, I found a variety of well-documented requirements and laws for these systems. Because these laws may differ by country, I will focus on the laws that I am used to: the German laws. You are not from Germany? No problem, these are the basics of a traffic light system that fulfills the requirements in Germany.

For pedestrians there are red and green lights with a little person who is either indicating to walk or to stop. We also have little traffic light men called Ampelmännchen in our capital Berlin. These are differently shaped traffic light men than you may find in the rest of the country. Yeah, you are right, I digress.

For vehicle drivers there are three colors: red, yellow, and green. The red and green lights have similar meaning as for pedestrians. The yellow light alone indicates that the traffic light is in the process of turning from green to red. This is a pre-cautious signal for drivers. Actually, you are not allowed to drive through a yellow traffic light, but few drivers abide by this law. If the red and yellow lights are shown together, the traffic light will shortly turn green. You are not allowed to drive yet, but you should be ready to move because this phase usually lasts only a partial second.

Concerning regulations, there is one hard rule: that at an intersection two traffic lights may never show green for both crossing directions. If this happens, the traffic light system has to shut down immediately. The system will turn to blinking yellow lights, thereby indicating that drivers have to take care of the traffic signs for who is allowed to drive now, or whether to grant other vehicles permission first. Our little traffic light controlling system has to take care of such error conditions as well. Right, I do not want to be involved in a car accident, just because the traffic control system showed green for two intersecting directions.

For traffic lights there are a variety of customizations in place. First, pedestrians may have to press a button in order to get a green light. The underlying controller will turn the traffic lights for the cars red first, then change the pedestrian lights to green—sometimes combined with a green signal for cars in the same direction depending on whether it's a traffic light at a crossing or a stand-alone pedestrian light. But most of the pedestrian lights are triggered together with the car lights without a necessary interaction from the pedestrian.

For some pedestrian crossings, the traffic light system might indicate a green walking sign together with an audible signal for the vision impaired. Shortly before turning red again, the acoustic signal will indicate that people should hurry to the other side of the street. The continuous signal will turn into an interrupted signal for the final five seconds of the green phase.

Another extension to the basic scenario are traffic lights with special signals— for example, at an intersection of two major routes, left-turning vehicles may get a green arrow on a different interval in order not to hinder the main traffic with long waiting periods. This can help traffic control a lot at heavy traffic crossings. But it also might lead to other problems in the traffic control system—especially when this is introduced together with a special traffic light for the right-turning vehicles as well (see Figure 5.1).

Yet another extension are induction loops that give the traffic lights a signal to turn green once a car arrives at a red light. The loop recognizes that a car has arrived, and the traffic light control system then schedules a green phase for that

Figure 5.1 A traffic light calling for some refactoring

newly arrived car. Another option are induction loops in a row to measure the driving speed and slow down speeders by turning the next signal red if the car is too fast. If that's not enough, imagine special radio signals sent to traffic light systems from ambulances, police cars, and busses that can turn traffic lights to green for their needs.

It seems that a traffic light system might look rather easy at first, but quickly turns into a complicated system. If our system should control the traffic lights of a major city, perhaps the mayor or public works director would be interested in usage statistics as well. With these he or she might be in the position to optimize the traffic flow based on the day and night time. Let's keep these possible evolution points in mind while developing the initial system. Right, we should make sure to implement the basic requirements before bringing in more features.

There are many large corporations now involved in building traffic management solutions. They acquire many various traffic data to optimize the flow through cities. The problem these companies are trying to solve is a very dynamic and complex one. A traffic light control system is one piece of such larger system. So, we will build a first piece for solving this problem.

FitNesse

In this part we will use FitNesse to define the specifications for the first steps of the traffic light system. FitNesse is a wiki system in which tests can be defined in a hierarchical way using wiki pages. Because FitNesse is a wiki, we can put additional information there, too. As the number of tests grows, we can grow the most relevant documentation along-side.

Since FitNesse is a wiki server, tests are defined using wiki notation. The FitNesse user guide[1] provides more information regarding the full markup language syntax. We will cover the essentials that you will need during this chapter. So, don't worry too much if you are unfamiliar with FitNesse or a wiki system.

FitNesse provides the ability to execute wiki pages as part of a test system. Initially, FitNesse was built as an extension to the Framework for Integrated Tests (FIT). Since 2008 it supports its own test system called SLiM–Simple List Invocation Method–which does not restrict the code used for test automation to the GPLv2 license as FIT does. You are right, we should define the traffic lights tests using the SLiM test notation and implementation rather than the FIT style.

In this example we will use two tables: the decision table and the scenario table. A decision table denotes input values to the system, executes some operation on the system under test, and checks some output values from the system. Input values and output values are denoted in a table in different rows. The notation is similar to the one we saw in the first part with Cucumber, and therefore quite intuitive to read. See, for example, the Valet Parking examples from the first part in a decision table in SLiM in Listing 5.1.

Listing 5.1 The Valet Parking tests expressed as a decision table in SLiM

```
 1  !|Parking costs for|Valet Parking  |
 2  |parking duration  |parking costs? |
 3  |30 minutes        |$ 12.00        |
 4  |3 hours           |$ 12.00        |
 5  |5 hours           |$ 12.00        |
 6  |5 hours 1 minute  |$ 18.00        |
 7  |12 hours          |$ 18.00        |
 8  |24 hours          |$ 18.00        |
 9  |1 day 1 minute    |$ 36.00        |
10  |3 days            |$ 54.00        |
11  |1 week            |$ 126.00       |
```

---

1. http://fitnesse.org/.FitNesse.UserGuide

A scenario table capsulates a common workflow more simply. You can think of it as a method or function that may accept parameters. We will describe different scenarios for different workflows that we will need. Scenario tables provide a way to abstract from lower-level details. We will keep our examples more readable with careful use of these scenario tables.

Supporting Code

In this part we will provide the production as well as the supporting code. The only difference from the airport example is that it will be developed using test-driven development. Since we are working in a Java example, we will use JUnit as unit test framework. Keep in mind that test automation is software development. We will apply guidelines for good code to the supporting code as well. After all, we can communicate our intent for the supporting code structure. Maintenance of the automated examples thereby becomes a no-brainer for whoever is going to maintain them—and this might be even you.

In JUnit we will use annotations to mark a method in a test class as a unit test (see line 4 in Listing 5.2). JUnit also provides assertions that ensure a certain state or behavior of the system or make the unit test fail if the behavior is not met. assertEquals(expected, actual) is the most used assertion (see line 6 in Listing 5.2). It checks that the expected value and the actual value are equal, or fails the test, providing a message that they mismatched.

Listing 5.2 An example of a unit test in Java

```
1  ...
2  public class LightStateTest {
3
4          @Test
5          public void testStateChange() {
6                  assertEquals(LightState.RED_YELLOW, LightState
        .RED.next());
7          }
8  }
```

As an advanced topic in JUnit, I will also use parameterized tests. These provide the possibility to separate the workflow and the tested data. The workflow is annotated as usual in a test method. The data for the tests is provided by a public static method with the proper annotation. We will work on this together as we reach this part of the problem.

Please note that a deeper introduction to JUnit is beyond the scope of this book. For more in-depth material on the topic *Test-driven Development by Example* [Bec02], *xUnit Test Patterns* [Mes07], and *Growing Object-oriented Software Guided by Tests* [FP09] are three references that I really enjoyed reading.

That should be everything we need to know in order to get started. Let's get going.

Summary

We dealt with the German traffic light rules for pedestrians and vehicle drivers. For pedestrians there are green and red lights; for vehicles, we have a series of green, yellow, red, red and yellow, and green state changes. When something goes wrong, our traffic controller will have to turn the traffic lights to yellow blinking.

I gave you a very brief overview over the automation framework and our approach to the support code. Did you install a Java IDE on your own and play around with it? Maybe you also took a look into FitNesse? Anyways, even if not, let's start with the implementation now. I will help you if necessary.

Chapter 6
Light States

W e are working toward a complete system of vehicle and crossing lights. We will also face the challenge that two driving directions will meet.

The first specification for a crossing will depend on the correct light state changes for cars. So, our first specification is built upon these charges. Our first test in FitNesse will be a decision table that yields the correct state transitions for cars. I will help you keep the basics covered. If you are looking for more in-depth material, check out Appendix B. In addition to a general introduction to FitNesse, I included links to more online material.

State Specifications

Let's start with a brief specification workshop. The state transition for a German traffic light system starts from the red light to the red and yellow lights. After that the light will turn green. From green it will turn yellow. The successor of the yellow light is the red light again. Oh, you're right, let's put them in a table (see Table 6.1).

Oh, you mean I forgot something? You're right. The invalid state is a yellow blinking light. Any malfunction in the system will turn the yellow light to blink. This is a cautious signal for all the vehicle drivers. Our system has to support this state and only a technician will manually bring the traffic light system out of this state. So far, we did not include this in our current table. Let's add this (see Table 6.2).

Table 6.1 Valid Light States for Cars

Previous State	Next State
red	red, yellow
red, yellow	green
green	yellow
yellow	red

Table 6.2 All Light States for Cars

Previous State	Next State
red	red, yellow
red, yellow	green
green	yellow
yellow	red
yellow blink	yellow blink

The First Test

Now let's get started with the first test. I downloaded the latest version of FitNesse from the distribution page[1] and stored it in the current folder. At the command line, I issue the command `java -jar fitnesse.jar -p 8080` in order to start FitNesse for the first time. In our current version of FitNesse, this unpacks the pages for an initial wiki. After printing out a lot of dots, it finishes unpacking the initial wiki (see Listing 6.1 for a sample) and starts the wiki-server. Now we may open the browser of our choice and point it to http://localhost:8080 to get the FitNesse entry page (see Figure 6.1).

Listing 6.1 Shell output from starting FitNesse for the first time

```
1  FitNesse (v20110104) Started...
2          port:              8080
3          root page:         fitnesse.wiki.FileSystemPage at
           ./FitNesseRoot
4          logger:            none
5          authenticator:     fitnesse.authentication.
           PromiscuousAuthenticator
6          html page factory: fitnesse.html.HtmlPageFactory
7          page version expiration set to 14 days.
```

As instructed by the startup screen, let's hit the edit button on the left, and add a line to the existing table for our traffic light test suite (see Listing 6.2). A test suite is a collection of test cases. We want to keep our tests separate from the remaining pages in the FitNesse wiki. That's why we start with a new, empty suite.

---

1. http://fitnesse.org

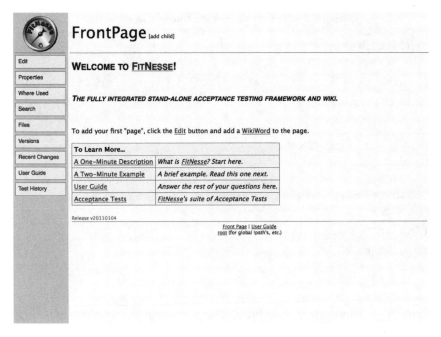

Figure 6.1 The FitNesse welcome screen when starting it for the first time

Listing 6.2 Adding a link to the FrontPage

```
1 | '''To Learn More...'''|
2 | [[A One-Minute Description][FitNesse.UserGuide.
    OneMinuteDescription]]|''What is [[FitNesse][FitNesse.
    FitNesse]]? Start here.''|
3 | [[A Two-Minute Example][FitNesse.UserGuide.TwoMinuteExample
    ]]|''A brief example. Read this one next.''|
4 | [[User Guide][FitNesse.UserGuide]]|''Answer the rest of your
     questions here.''|
5 | [[Acceptance Tests][FitNesse.SuiteAcceptanceTests]]|''
    FitNesse's suite of Acceptance Tests''|
6 | [[Traffic Light System][TrafficLights]]|''Traffic Light
    System Acceptance Tests''|
```

After saving the page, our new Traffic Light system appears in the table, but
with an ending question mark to it. The question mark indicates that the page does
not yet exist. Let's click on the question mark to get to an edit window where we
can edit our new page TrafficLights. Let's put in the contents of Listing 6.3.

Listing 6.3 The root suite of the traffic light examples

```
 1  !1 Traffic Lights control system
 2
 3  This suite consists of a set of tests for the traffic lights
       control system.
 4
 5  ----
 6  !contents -R2 -g -p -f -h
 7
 8  !*< SLiM relevant stuff
 9
10  !define TEST_SYSTEM {slim}
11  !path classes
12
13  *!
```

Lines 1 to 3 indicate a little bit of documentation for our traffic light suite. Below the four dashes the table of contents is created automatically by FitNesse (line 6). The remaining lines are a hidden section that indicate that we want to use SLiM to describe our test tables and that additional helper classes can be loaded from the classes folder.[2] After saving the page contents, we have to switch to the properties page by clicking the button with that label and change the page type to suite. After saving it, we can run this suite by pressing the suite button, although it will fail since we haven't added any tests to the suite.

Our first test will be about traffic light states, but our next tests will deal with controlling different states for a crossing. Having this knowledge, let's organize our tests into two suites: one for crossing controls and another one for traffic light states. We create the first page by clicking on the "add child" link on the top of the page, selecting Suite as page type, naming the new page TrafficLightStates, and leaving the default page content as is. We will change the default content in a few moments to add some documentation to it as well. When hitting the add button, the table of contents for the TrafficLights suite adds the TrafficLightStates page, the page we just created. We click on the link to the TrafficLightStates page.

---

2. In the strict TDD world we could now philosophize whether I added something without having a failing test first. Having worked with FitNesse for the past three years or so, I am confident in knowing what I am doing here to the degree that I still feel safe and I am certain that I will use the last two definitions for the classpath and the test system later. Such arguments for a more pedantic application of TDD make sense in some contexts. In our context I will try to be pragmatic as long as I still feel safe with my assumptions, knowing that we can recover later if we lose that feeling.

Let's hit the edit button to change the default page contents to a more meaningful description. Let's start with a similar description as in the upper suite (see Listing 6.4).

Listing 6.4 The contents of the TrafficLightStates suite

```
1 !1 States of traffic lights
2
3 This suite exercises different traffic light states.
4
5 ----
6 !contents -R2 -g -p -f -h
```

Finally, we can add a test page to the TrafficLightState suite called CarTraffic-States. We do this similarly to the way we added the TrafficLightStates page to the TrafficLights suite. The only difference is that we select Test as page type this time. After opening the newly created CarTrafficState page, we can start thinking about the first test. Let's take a look at our specification (see Table 6.2).

We want to express the state transitions as we identified them during our workshop. The table looks like a decision table in SLiM. In a decision table we write down test cases line by line. Any column whose header does not end with a question mark expresses an input value to the system; any column whose header ends with a question mark expresses an output from the system, which will be checked. For our traffic light state transitions, we need a decision table with one input value–the previous state of the light, i.e., its color–and one checked outcome value–the next state or color. Let's write down the first line of the table with the state transition from red to red and yellow (see Listing 6.5).

Listing 6.5 The first test expressing a state transition from red to red and yellow

```
1 !|Traffic Lights            |
2 |previous state|next state? |
3 |red           |red, yellow |
```

This test expresses the transition from the red light – indicating that cars stop–to the red and yellow state–indicating that the lights will turn green in a few seconds. After saving this first test, let's execute it. FitNesse tells us that some classes are missing. Figure 6.2 shows the output.

FitNesse tells us that we should start the Java editor of our choice and get some classes implemented.

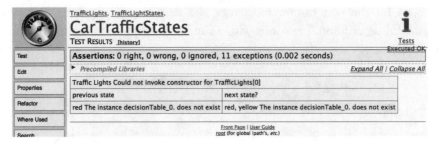

Figure 6.2 The FitNesse result from the first test run

Diving into the Code

Before I start to explain how we will develop the supporting code, let's take a look on the current folder layout to find out how to set up our IDE. The folder layout of the traffic lights project so far consists of `fitnesse.jar` and a folder—`FitNesseRoot`—that contains the wiki pages for FitNesse. In the root suite for our traffic lights system we added the statement `!path classes`, which indicates that FitNesse shall put any classes from the folder `classes` onto its classpath while executing the tests. So, our classes should get compiled into the `classes` folder parallel to `fitnesse.jar`. Following common practice for Java code, the source code will be stored in a folder called `src` parallel to the `(FitNesseRoot)` folder. With this setup we can configure our IDE for this project.[3]

The first failing test told us that we need to create a class called TrafficLights with a parameter-less constructor. The numbers in square brackets indicate the number of parameters a constructor or function gets. We create this class in the default package (see Listing 6.6).

Listing 6.6 The first support code class

```
1 public class TrafficLights {
2
3 }
```

Since the default constructor does not take any parameters in Java by default, we are done for now. As we set up our IDE to automatically compile changes for us to the classes folder, we may directly rerun the test in FitNesse in order to see if

---

3. Please note that an introduction to a Java IDE is beyond the scope of this book. There are great resources online for this. I used eclipse in the github project (http://github.com/mgaertne/trafficlights) to do that, but it should be straightforward for the other IDEs out there.

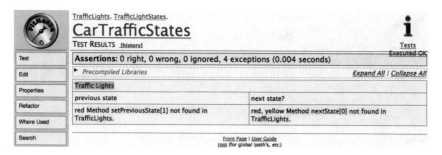

Figure 6.3 The FitNesse result after creating the class

our assumptions were correct and for FitNesse to tell us about the next functions that we should implement. The result (see Figure 6.3) shows us that FitNesse now found the class and expects two more methods: setPreviousState, which gets a parameter, and the parameter-less nextState method.

The left-hand column labelled "previous state" stores some value into the system in order to prepare the initial state of the traffic light. So the method setPreviousState takes one parameter, the value from the table. The nextState method on the other hand is expected to return a value that is then checked by FitNesse against the value in the table. So, in order to make progress, we add these two methods with an empty body to the TrafficLights class (see Listing 6.7).

Listing 6.7 The support code class with empty method bodies

```
1  public class TrafficLights {
2
3      public void setPreviousState(String state) {
4
5      }
6
7      public String nextState() {
8          return null;
9      }
10 }
```

When we rerun our test in FitNesse, we can see that we finally made some progress as the test turned from yellow—indicating exceptions or missing code—to red—indicating that something went wrong (see Figure 6.4).

At this point we need to start developing the algorithm. We do this by returning a hard-coded string for the first test.

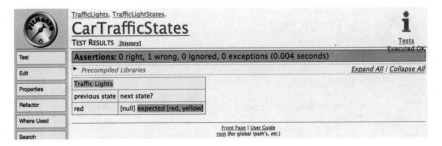

Figure 6.4 The FitNesse test has now turned from yellow to red—we made progress

Listing 6.8 The return value of the nextState method is hard-coded

```
1  public class TrafficLights {
2
3  ...
4         public String nextState() {
5                 return ''red, yellow'';
6         }
7  }
```

When executing the test again, it is passing now (see Figure 6.5). This indicates that it's time to check in these results to the source control system—everything including the sources as well as the `FitNesseRoot`.

Now, we can continue adding the next test. Let's add the second line from the specification table. This contains the transition from red and yellow to green (see Listing 6.9). Running this test gives us a red test again, because the output value does not match the expected one.

In order to make this test pass, we need to remember the original state. Based upon this previous state, we need to decide what to do in the function for the next

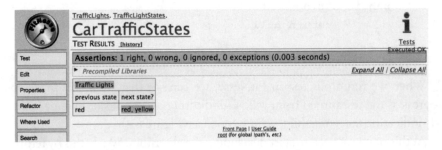

Figure 6.5 The first example is now passing

Listing 6.9 The second test expressing a state transition from red and yellow to green

```
1 !|Traffic Lights            |
2 |previous state|next state? |
3 |red            |red, yellow |
4 |red, yellow    |green       |
```

state. We can achieve this by remembering the state in a String field, and adding an if to the nextState function (see Listing 6.10).

Listing 6.10 Deciding based upon the previous state which one to return

```
1 public class TrafficLights {
2
3          private String state;
4
5          public void setPreviousState(String state) {
6                  this.state = state;
7          }
8
9          public String nextState() {
10                 if (''red''.equals(state)) return
11                     ''red, yellow,'';
12                 return ''green'';
13         }
14 }
```

Again we execute the tests and see that they pass. This indicates a check-in time to the source control repository for us.

Now, because the second test is passing, let's add the remaining transitions in the same manner. We can update the code along the way. Let's start with the remaining three tests to end up with the table in Listing 6.11.

Listing 6.11 The final test table for car states

```
1 !|Traffic Lights            |
2 |previous state|next state? |
3 |red            |red, yellow |
4 |red, yellow    |green       |
5 |green          |yellow      |
6 |yellow         |red         |
7 |invalid state  |yellow blink|
```

Please note that we also added a state representing an invalid configuration where the yellow lights will blink.

In order to make this pass, we can add some more if statements in the nextState function. This yields the results as in Listing 6.12.

Listing 6.12 The first flow after implementing all light configurations

```
 1 public class TrafficLights {
 2 ...
 3         public String nextState() {
 4                 if (''red''.equals(state)) return ''red,
        yellow'';
 5                 if (''red, yellow''.equals(state)) return ''
        green'';
 6                 if (''green''.equals(state)) return ''yellow'';
 7                 if (''yellow''.equals(state)) return ''red'';
 8                 return ''yellow blink'';
 9         }
10 ...
```

We re-execute the tests to see that they are still passing. Everything fine? Then let's check in the changes.

Refactoring

At this point we could move on to the next implementation function and the next examples. But we're certainly not done yet. There are two flaws that I am unhappy with, and we should be responsible for cleaning up the mess we made. In addition, moving on without correcting the flaws would not make much sense.

First, we implemented everything in the source class that shall glue together the production code and the tests. So, in order to be really finished, we need to peel this code out into a new class or concept of our production code. Ideally, we do this using test-driven development (TDD) [Bec02]. We will first write one tiny test, then execute it to see it really fails, implementing just enough to make this test pass, then refactor. Does this remind you of the cycle for the parking lot example? Exactly, but we will work on a smaller fragment of the code than we did with the specification.

We will implement the new code in a parallel class. This is called a parallel component, and we will implement it in parallel to the existing code. Later we can exchange the support code with its hard-coded values for our new domain code. If we see the acceptance tests still passing, we know that we did everything right.

The second flaw I am unhappy about is the fact that we developed all our code in the default package. That's bad, because we really should have a place for this code when the code base starts to grow. Since this step is easy, let's start with this one.

Packages

Moving a class into some package is nowadays a no-brainer in most development environments using the right tools. This is such a basic refactoring that it's incorporated into any IDE, and nearly every programmer either uses this intuitively through drag and drop or knows where to find it. But we still need to know how to tell FitNesse how to find the classes in the new package. An import table does the trick. In an import table we list packages from which we want to use support code classes. We can add multiple lines indicating that we are going to use classes from multiple packages in our test. We put the TrafficLights class into the package `org.trafficlights.test.acceptance` and add the import table on top of the CarTrafficState page, resulting in the content from Listing 6.13.

Listing 6.13 The final example page after the refactoring

```
1  !|import                          |
2  |org.trafficlights.test.acceptance|
3
4  !|Traffic Lights               |
5  |previous state|next state? |
6  |red            |red, yellow |
7  |red, yellow    |green       |
8  |green          |yellow      |
9  |yellow         |red         |
10 |invalid state  |yellow blink|
```

After refactoring the code and adding the import table, we run the test. It passes, so it is time for us to check in these changes.

The LightState Enum

The next changes will involve changing only the code. We will grow a separate class from our support code and then change the implementation of the support code to use our new class. We do this by driving a new design. The car state handling looks like an enumeration to me. Let's start to drive the implementation of an enum class in Java. Of course, we do this using TDD for our production code.

The first step using TDD is a failing JUnit test. We take the data from our first acceptance test for this, which is the state change from red to red and yellow. So, the first unit test shall express this state transition. We will call the enumeration LightState in the `org.trafficlights.domain` package, and it will have one function called `next()`, which returns the next light state. In the design pattern literature this is called a State Pattern [GHJV94]. Our first unit test to drive this implementation is the one in Listing 6.14.

Listing 6.14 The first unit test driving the domain concept of a LightState

```
1  package org.trafficlights.domain;
2
3  import static org.junit.Assert.*;
4
5  import org.junit.Test;
6
7  public class LightStateTest {
8
9          @Test
10         public void testStateChange() {
11                 assertEquals(LightState.RED_YELLOW, LightState
       .RED.next());
12         }
13 }
```

The assertion in line 11 states that the next state of the RED state shall be equal to the RED_YELLOW state. The function `assertEquals` takes two arguments: the expected value first (RED_YELLOW) and the actual value second (RED).

Since the class LightState does not exist, we create it as an enumeration in the same package and add the values RED and RED_YELLOW together with the abstract function `next()` to it (see Listing 6.15).

Listing 6.15 The first code base for the new traffic light enum

```
1  public enum LightState {
2          RED {
3                  public LightState next() { return null; }
4          },
5          RED_YELLOW {
6                  public LightState next() { return null; }
7          };
```

```
 8
 9        public abstract LightState next();
10
11 }
```

The unit test is now compilable, and we can run it for the first time. Doing so results in a red bar indicating that the result is not the right one. Upon analysis we notice that the next() function for the RED state returns null rather than RED_YELLOW. We change this by returning RED_YELLOW from RED's next() function as in Listing 6.16.

Listing 6.16 The first implementation for the LightState transition from RED to RED_YELLOW

```
 1 public enum LightState {
 2        RED {
 3                public LightState next() { return RED_YELLOW; }
 4        },
 5        RED_YELLOW {
 6                public LightState next() { return null; }
 7        };
 8
 9        public abstract LightState next();
10
11 }
```

Executing the unit test again turns it green. Rerunning our FitNesse test tells us that we can safely check in our work now. Let's do that.

The next state transitions from the acceptance test are straightforward. The transition from RED_YELLOW to GREEN is very similar to the one from RED to RED_YELLOW. Figuring that all the remaining tests will be similar, I propose to implement a parameterized test for these state changes (see Listing 6.17).

Listing 6.17 The first and second unit test expressed as a data-driven test using the Parameterized runner from JUnit

```
 1 package org.trafficlights.domain;
 2
 3 import static java.util.Arrays.*;
 4 import static org.junit.Assert.*;
 5 import static org.trafficlights.domain.LightState.*;
```

```
 6
 7 import java.util.List;
 8
 9 import org.junit.Test;
10 import org.junit.runner.RunWith;
11 import org.junit.runners.Parameterized;
12 import org.junit.runners.Parameterized.Parameters;
13
14 @RunWith(Parameterized.class)
15 public class LightStateTest {
16
17        @Parameters
18        public static List<Object[]> data() {
19                return asList(new Object[][] {
20                        { RED, RED_YELLOW },
21                        { RED_YELLOW, GREEN }
22                });
23        }
24
25        private LightState previousState;
26        private LightState nextState;
27
28        public LightStateTest(LightState previousState,
      LightState nextState) {
29                this.previousState = previousState;
30                this.nextState = nextState;
31        }
32
33        @Test
34        public void testStateChange() {
35                assertEquals(nextState, previousState.next());
36        }
37 }
```

In a parameterized test in JUnit the class is annotated to use the Parameterized test runner (see line 14). There is also one annotated static function that returns the parameters to pass to this class (see line 18). The constructor takes these values as parameters (see line 28) and stores them to fields on that class. The test method can then assert against the fields rather than local variables.

We can make this test compilable adding the new value GREEN to the enum, implementing the next() function by returning null. Running the test, we see it failing, and we can make it pass by returning GREEN from RED_YELLOW's next() method (see line 8 in Listing 6.18).

Listing 6.18 The second transition is now captured

```
1  package org.trafficlights.domain;
2
3  public enum LightState {
4          RED {
5                  public LightState next() { return RED_YELLOW; }
6          },
7          RED_YELLOW {
8                  public LightState next() { return GREEN; }
9          },
10         GREEN {
11                 public LightState next() { return null; }
12         };
13
14         public abstract LightState next();
15
16 }
```

When we run the tests, the green bar indicates that we should check in these changes to the version control system.

We can drive the transition from GREEN to YELLOW and YELLOW to RED in the same way, ending up with the tests as shown in Listing 6.19 and the code as shown in Listing 6.20: We should not forget to check in the results each time we have a green bar.

Listing 6.19 All four light states covered

```
1  package org.trafficlights.domain;
2
3  ...
4
5  @RunWith(Parameterized.class)
6  public class LightStateTest {
7
8          @Parameters
```

```
9              public static List<Object[]> data() {
10                  return asList(new Object[][] {
11                          { RED, RED_YELLOW },
12                          { RED_YELLOW, GREEN },
13                          { GREEN, YELLOW },
14                          { YELLOW, RED }
15                  });
16          }
17 ...
18 }
```

Listing 6.20 The four light states covered in the code

```
1 package org.trafficlights.domain;
2
3 public enum LightState {
4      RED {
5              public LightState next() { return RED_YELLOW; }
6      },
7      RED_YELLOW {
8              public LightState next() { return GREEN; }
9      },
10     GREEN {
11             public LightState next() { return YELLOW; }
12     },
13     YELLOW {
14             public LightState next() { return RED; }
15     };
16
17     public abstract LightState next();
18
19 }
```

Now, for the final test from our FitNesse support code we need to add one more value to the enum, which is the unknown value. By default the next() function should return the UNKNOWN value. Thereby we will be fulfilling the requirements from the German law, that the traffic light should start to blink if there is a misconfiguration. We drive this implementation again with a unit test (see Listing 6.21).

Listing 6.21 All four light states covered, and the blinking yellow requirement fulfilled

```
1  package org.trafficlights.domain;
2
3  ...
4
5  @RunWith(Parameterized.class)
6  public class LightStateTest {
7
8          @Parameters
9          public static List<Object[]> data() {
10                 return asList(new Object[][] {
11                             { RED, RED_YELLOW },
12                             { RED_YELLOW, GREEN },
13                             { GREEN, YELLOW },
14                             { YELLOW, RED },
15                             { UNKNOWN, UNKNOWN }
16                     });
17         }
18
19 ...
```

We make this test compiling by adding the UNKNOWN value to the LightState class and making the next() method concrete by returning UNKOWN for any enum value which does not implement next() itself (see Listing 6.22).

Listing 6.22 The final implementation covering all states our traffic light needs

```
1  package org.trafficlights.domain;
2
3  public enum LightState {
4          RED {
5                  public LightState next() { return RED_YELLOW;
6          },
7          RED_YELLOW {
8                  public LightState next() { return GREEN; }
9          },
10         GREEN {
11                 public LightState next() { return YELLOW; }
```

```
12              },
13              YELLOW {
14                      public LightState next() { return RED; }
15              },
16              UNKNOWN;
17
18              public LightState next() {
19                      return UNKNOWN;
20              }
21
22  }
```

When we run these tests, the green bar indicates that we can check in our changes.

Editing LightStates

We test-drove our component in parallel to the supporting code that our FitNesse test uses. We now need to change the support code to make use of our new enumeration. Unfortunately, the FitNesse test deals with strings, and we need to translate them into one of the values from the LightState enumeration. We could put a rather large if-then-elseif-else construct into the support code. This does not sound like a good design, though. Let's avoid such complication in the code—especially in the support code, which should be kept simple. Instead, FitNesse offers the possibility to convert strings to domain objects using property editors. The property editor will take care to convert one value into a string, and convert the value back.

We can achieve this by naming our property editor class after the domain class that we want to convert with the suffix Editor. For our LightState class we need to implement a class called LightStateEditor. We have to subclass this from PropertyEditorSupport and implement the methods getAsText() and setAsText(String).[4] Again, we test-drive our implementation of the Light-StateEditor class. The first unit test checks that invoking setAsText with the string "red" stores the LightState RED into the editor (see Listing 6.23).

---

4. You should also check the FitNesse UserGuide on this: http://fitnesse.org/FitNesse
.UserGuide.SliM.CustomTypes.

Listing 6.23 The unit test for setting the value to red

```
1  public class LightStateEditorTest {
2
3       private LightStateEditor editor = new LightStateEditor
    ();
4
5       @Test
6       public void setRed() {
7               editor.setAsText(''red'');
8               assertEquals(LightState.RED, editor.getValue());
9       }
10 }
```

In order to make this test pass, we will create the class LightStateEditor deriving from PropertyEditorSupport, implement the setAsText() method, and call setValue with the RED state unconditionally (see Listing 6.24).

Listing 6.24 The first implementation of the LightStateEditor

```
1  package org.trafficlights.domain;
2
3  import java.beans.PropertyEditorSupport;
4
5  public class LightStateEditor extends PropertyEditorSupport {
6
7          public void setAsText(String state) {
8                  setValue(LightState.RED);
9          }
10 }
```

After checking in this code, we can transform the unit test into a data-driven test using JUnit's Parameterized runner again. Adding the next conversion from "red, yellow" to the right enum value leads to the unit test in Listing 6.25.

Listing 6.25 The second unit test using a data driven format

```
1  @RunWith(Parameterized.class)
2  public class LightStateEditorTest {
3
4          @Parameters
```

```
 5          public static List<Object[]> data() {
 6                  return asList(new Object[][] {
 7                                  { ''red'', RED },
 8                                  { ''red, yellow'', RED_YELLOW }
 9                  });
10          }
11
12          private LightStateEditor editor = new LightStateEditor
    ();
13          private String stateName;
14          private LightState state;
15
16          public LightStateEditorTest(String stateName,
    LightState state) {
17                  this.stateName = stateName;
18                  this.state = state;
19          }
20
21          @Test
22          public void setAsText() {
23                  editor.setAsText(stateName);
24                  assertEquals(state, editor.getValue());
25          }
26 }
```

The new test can be made green by adding a conditional statement to the editor code (see Listing 6.26).

Listing 6.26 A conditional to the rescue for the red and yellow state

```
1          public void setAsText(String state) {
2                  if (''red''.equals(state)) {
3                          setValue(LightState.RED);
4                          return;
5                  }
6                  setValue(LightState.RED_YELLOW);
7          }
```

After checking this progress in, I get a bit concerned about the direction we are heading in. Let's think about the next test for a second. The setting of the green state will be straightforward based on the previous examples.

Making the test for the state conversion of the green state pass, I recognize that we added a second if statement to the editor code. At this point our code seems to become worse and worse. So, let's take a different approach to implement the editor, refactoring the implementation up to that point.

First we need to make the unit test pass by including the mentioned second if statement (see Listing 6.27).

Listing 6.27 Strike three for duplication indicates the refactoring potential for this code

```
1  public void setAsText(String state) {
2                  if (''red''.equals(state)) {
3                          setValue(LightState.RED);
4                          return;
5                  }
6                  if (''red, yellow''.equals(state)) {
7                          setValue(LightState.RED_YELLOW);
8                          return;
9                  }
10                 setValue(LightState.GREEN);
11         }
```

After seeing the green bar and checking in the code to the version control repository, let's refactor the LightState enumeration, so that the constructor takes a String parameter for the description of the state (see Listing 6.28).

Listing 6.28 The LightState now takes a String parameter for the description in the constructor

```
1  public enum LightState {
2  ...
3          String description;
4
5          private LightState() {
6                  this('''');
7          }
8
9          private LightState(String description) {
10                 this.description = description;
```

```
11            }
12 ...
13 }
```

In order to keep the code compiling, we also need to introduce an explicit default constructor. We need to make the field `description` visible to the editor in the same package. Now, we can remove the duplication, replacing the code for the RED state in the editor with a loop over all the values in the LightState enumeration, checking for a match of the passed in parameter with the description and setting the value if they match (see Listing 6.29).

Listing 6.29 Iterating over all the values in LightState to check for a matching description

```
1 public class LightStateEditor extends PropertyEditorSupport {
2
3        public void setAsText(String state) {
4                if (''red''.equals(state)) {
5                        setValue(LightState.RED);
6                        return;
7                }
8                if (''red, yellow''.equals(state)) {
9                        setValue(LightState.RED_YELLOW);
10                       return;
11               }
12               setValue(LightState.GREEN);
13
14               for (LightState lightState: LightState.values
       ()) {
15                       if (lightState.description.equals(
       state)) {
16                               setValue(lightState);
17                               return;
18                       }
19               }
20       }
21 }
```

Now, we can replace the declaration of the RED state with a call to the constructor taking the description as an argument (see Listing 6.30).

Listing 6.30 The red state makes use of the description field

```
1  public enum LightState {
2          RED(''red'') {
3  ...
4  }
```

Seeing all the tests still passing,[5] we can take out the first two lines in the
setAsText function of the editor. The loop should step in now. We repeat the
same process for the values of RED_YELLOW and GREEN, thereby reducing the
setAsText function effectively to the loop (see Listing 6.31).

Listing 6.31 The property editor in its shortest form

```
1  public class LightStateEditor extends PropertyEditorSupport {
2
3          public void setAsText(String state) {
4                  for (LightState lightState: LightState.values
       ()) {
5                          if (lightState.description.equals(
       state)) {
6                                  setValue(lightState);
7                                  return;
8                          }
9                  }
10         }
11 }
```

After checking this fragment in, we continue to add the tests for the YELLOW
state, and also add the UNKNOWN value to the data-driven test. In the end we
also add a unit test for defaulting the state to the blinking yellow light when no
proper LightState value could be found during the iteration. As a final cleanup we
may drop the parameter-less constructor from the LightState class completely as it
is no longer needed. The resulting code for the unittest, editor code, and LightState
enumeration can be found in Listings 6.32, 6.33, and 6.34 respectively.

---

5. I hope you figured that we can run both the unit tests as well as the acceptance tests at this point.

Listing 6.32 The unit tests for the editor after finishing the implementation for setAsText

```
1  @RunWith(Parameterized.class)
2  public class LightStateEditorTest {
3
4          @Parameters
5          public static List<Object[]> data() {
6                  return asList(new Object[][] {
7                                  { ''red'', RED },
8                                  { ''red, yellow'', RED_YELLOW },
9                                  { ''green'', GREEN },
10                                 { ''yellow'', YELLOW },
11                                 { ''yellow blink'', UNKNOWN },
12                                 { ''invalid state'', UNKNOWN }
13                  });
14         }
15
16         private LightStateEditor editor = new LightStateEditor
       ();
17         private String stateName;
18         private LightState state;
19
20         public LightStateEditorTest(String stateName,
       LightState state) {
21                 this.stateName = stateName;
22                 this.state = state;
23         }
24
25         @Test
26         public void setAsText() {
27                 editor.setAsText(stateName);
28                 assertEquals(state, editor.getValue());
29         }
30 }
```

Listing 6.33 The LightStateEditor code after driving the implementation for setAsText

```
1  public class LightStateEditor extends PropertyEditorSupport {
2
3          public void setAsText(String state) {
4                  for (LightState lightState: LightState.values
      ()) {
5                          if (lightState.description.equals(
      state)) {
6                                  setValue(lightState);
7                                  return;
8                          }
9                  }
10                 setValue(LightState.UNKNOWN);
11         }
12 }
```

Listing 6.34 The code for the LightState enumeration after implementing the first method on the editor

```
1  public enum LightState {
2          RED(''red'') {
3                  public LightState next() { return RED_YELLOW;
      }
4          },
5          RED_YELLOW(''red, yellow'') {
6                  public LightState next() { return GREEN; }
7          },
8          GREEN(''green'') {
9                  public LightState next() { return YELLOW; }
10         },
11         YELLOW(''yellow'') {
12                 public LightState next() { return RED; }
13         },
14         UNKNOWN(''yellow blink'');
15
16         String description;
17
18         private LightState(String description) {
19                 this.description = description;
```

```
20                }
21
22                public LightState next() {
23                        return UNKNOWN;
24                }
25
26 }
```

With the unit test now in place, we can start driving the second method for FitNesse, which is the getAsText() method. We will reuse our data-driven unit test, since we will deal mostly with the same values. I add another test method to my data-driven unit test class for the getAsText() function (see Listing 6.35).

Listing 6.35 The unit test for the getAsText function in the LightStateEditor

```
 1 @RunWith(Parameterized.class)
 2 public class LightStateEditorTest {
 3
 4 ...
 5        @Test
 6        public void getAsText() {
 7                editor.setValue(state);
 8                assertEquals(stateName, editor.getAsText());
 9        }
10 }
```

Running the tests for the first time, they fail since the default implementation of getAsText() does not provide the expected results. Let's add the getAsText() implementation to the LightStateEditor, which gets the stored value first, casts it to a LightState, and returns the description of the state (see Listing 6.36).

Listing 6.36 The code for the getAsText method in LightStateEditor

```
1 public class LightStateEditor extends PropertyEditorSupport {
2 ...
3        public String getAsText() {
4                LightState state = (LightState) getValue();
5                return state.description;
6        }
7 }
```

When we execute the tests now, there is something surprising to me. The last unit test checks for defaulting of any arbitrary string to the unknown value. Since this test failure is unexpected, I start to think over the design so far. We put the responsibility for knowing about the next state in line into the state class. While driving the editor for hooking up our new domain concept into FitNesse we put the responsibility to default to the unknown state into the editor. Is this responsibility in the right place?

Reconsidering the requirements, I propose to put the responsibility for falling back to the UNKNOWN value into the enum class, since we are likely to need it later in order to show law fulfillments in our domain classes. Therefore, we need to extract from the setAsText function a method that gets a string parameter and returns a LightState for that string. This sounds like a valueFor function to me. Let's make it public static and put it on the LightState enum (see Listing 6.37 and Listing 6.38).

Listing 6.37 The extracted body from the LightStateEditor as valueFor on the LightState class

```
1 public enum LightState {
2 ...
3           public static LightState valueFor(String stateName) {
4                   for (LightState state: values()) {
5                           if (state.description.equals(stateName
   )) return state;
6                   }
7                   return UNKNOWN;
8           }
9
10 ...
11 }
```

Listing 6.38 The changed implementation of the editor class

```
1 public class LightStateEditor extends PropertyEditorSupport {
2 ...
3           public void setAsText(String state) {
4                   setValue(LightState.valueFor(state));
5           }
6 ...
7 }
```

These changes still don't make the tests pass, but it is now obvious to me that the tests no longer test the editor behavior, but the LightState enumeration. Can you also spot it? In order to communicate our intention to the next person maintaining this code—and that might also be either of us—we should rename the test classes we have so far. The LightStateTest becomes the new LightStateTransitionTest, and the LightStateEditorTest is reduced by the defaulting test (see Listing 6.39). Finally, for the new `valueFor()` method, we introduce a new data-driven test, LightStateTest, which checks for the correct defaulting behavior (see Listing 6.40).

Listing 6.39 The unit test for the editor with the defaulting behavior unit test removed

```
1  @RunWith(Parameterized.class)
2  public class LightStateEditorTest {
3
4          @Parameters
5          public static List<Object[]> data() {
6                  return asList(new Object[][] {
7                                       { ''red'', RED },
8                                       { ''red, yellow'', RED_YELLOW },
9                                       { ''green'', GREEN },
10                                      { ''yellow'', YELLOW },
11                                      { ''yellow blink'', UNKNOWN }
12                  });
13         }
14  ...
15  }
```

Listing 6.40 The new unit test class for the valueFor method

```
1  package org.trafficlights.domain;
2
3  import static java.util.Arrays.*;
4  import static org.junit.Assert.*;
5  import static org.trafficlights.domain.LightState.*;
6
7  import java.util.List;
8
9  import org.junit.Test;
10  import org.junit.runner.RunWith;
```

```
11 import org.junit.runners.Parameterized;
12 import org.junit.runners.Parameterized.Parameters;
13
14 @RunWith(Parameterized.class)
15 public class LightStateTest {
16
17         @Parameters
18         public static List<Object[]> data() {
19                 return asList(new Object[][] {
20                                 { ''red'', RED },
21                                 { ''red, yellow'', RED_YELLOW },
22                                 { ''green'', GREEN },
23                                 { ''yellow'', YELLOW },
24                                 { ''yellow blink'', UNKNOWN },
25                                 { ''invalid value'', UNKNOWN }
26                 });
27         }
28
29         private String stateName;
30         private LightState state;
31
32         public LightStateTest(String stateName, LightState
       state) {
33                 this.stateName = stateName;
34                 this.state = state;
35         }
36
37         @Test
38         public void valueFor() {
39                 assertEquals(state, LightState.valueFor(
       stateName));
40         }
41
42 }
```

Seeing that all unit tests now pass, we may check in all of these changes to the version control system. We are nearly done for now. The last step is to make use of the new enumeration in our support code class. Let's open the TrafficLights class and change the signature of the setPreviousState() method to take a LightState type, change the type of the state field to LightState accordingly, and change the nextState method to return state.next() as a LightState (see Listing 6.41).

Listing 6.41 The final TrafficLights implementation making use of our domain concept of a LightState

```
 1 package org.trafficlights.test.acceptance;
 2
 3 import org.trafficlights.domain.LightState;
 4
 5 public class TrafficLights {
 6
 7        private LightState state;
 8
 9        public void setPreviousState(LightState state) {
10                this.state = state;
11        }
12
13        public LightState nextState() {
14                return state.next();
15        }
16 }
```

Let's go back to the browser and execute the FitNesse test. Because it still passes, we can check in everything and give ourselves a high-five. Do you see how much simpler the support code just became? The missing domain concept helped us a lot here. Let's head to the coffee machine for a break.

Summary

During the break, let's revisit what we did so far. We introduced a state with a transition map for different light states. We drove the domain concept from the acceptance tests and added a bunch of unit tests for that as well. Finally, we added an editor for the new domain concept and hooked everything up to the existing acceptance test. Quite a bunch of insights that we got during the last few minutes.

By noticing what the tests try to make us aware of, we noticed a problem with our understanding of the problem domain. After putting the responsibility for defaulting to a proper LightState to the LightState class, the support code became way simpler. One of the advantages of driving the application from the outside-in through acceptance tests reveals concepts missing in the domain code. If we were retrofitting the tests to some existing code base, we would have to revisit the whole application while automating the tests, effectively making the code more testable. When working from the acceptance criteria toward the design, we can notice such design flaws way earlier, when changes to the design are more easy. Since no one based other classes on our suboptimal domain classes, we were more flexible to introduce such changes. Clearly, at this point we saved a bunch of programmers many hours by avoiding to force everyone to come up with some defaulting logic on their own. "Good job" you say? Yes, you are right about that.

Chapter 7
First Crossing

In this chapter we want to deal with the first thing for a traffic lights control system. Assume we have two crossing roads, and the most basic thing for our system will be to control the traffic lights for each direction. There is one thing the law asks us to consider for this system: Two crossing directions are never under any circumstance allowed to show green at the same time. We will keep this in mind while coming up with examples for our controller.

Controller Specifications

Let's take a look at the specifications for the controller. We have two directions. The controller controls state transitions, probably by transitioning to the next state when some timer expires. The controller will change just one light at a time. For example, if the traffic light shows green for one direction and red for another one, then the controller changes the first direction to yellow before the red one is changed to red and yellow. Otherwise, we would enter an invalid state.

Thus we can simplify our controller to the case where we change one light at a time. We have to consider two previous light states for the two directions and will get two light states afterwards. We can assume that our controller changes just the first of the two states.

Let's look at the valid transitions first, what I refer to as the happy path scenario. Most of my specifications start from this. When we have two red lights and change the first light then we will end up in red and yellow for the first light and red for the second light. After that, the controller will transition the red and yellow first light to the green state. The second light is kept red. From green we transition back to yellow and finally to red. We might end up with a table similar to the one in Table 7.1.

Let's consider the invalid states next. Thinking through the remaining cases, I start to realize that any other case will lead to an invalid state, and I want the controller to switch to the blinking light then. Since the first light can change only when the second shows red, any other combination is invalid and will lead to a car

Table 7.1 Happy Path Scenario for Controller State Transitions

First Light	Second Light	Next First Light	Next Second Light
red	red	red, yellow	red
red, yellow	red	green	red
green	red	yellow	red
yellow	red	red	red

Table 7.2 All Controller State Transitions we have to Consider

First Light	Second Light	Next First Light	Next Second Light
red	red	red, yellow	red
red, yellow	red	green	red
green	red	yellow	red
yellow	red	red	red
in any	other case	yellow blink	yellow blink

accident if we don't take care of it. For example, while the yellow light shows for the second direction, we shall not be allowed to change to anything other than red. If we changed to green, cars from the yellow direction could still pass the light. So, we can take a note on this in our table (see Table 7.2).

With these pre-thoughts, let's start with the implementation of the controller.

Driving the Controller

So far we have built traffic light colors as states in the system. As before, we will start with a test inside FitNesse. We will again start with the first acceptance criteria.

Let's start the first test by creating a new suite called CrossingControl in FitNesse. We add the test page TwoCarCrossings to the new suite. In order to drive the behavior, we will focus on the happy path tests first. So, when one direction shows the green light and the second one shows red, when the green light changes to the next state, we should expect the green light to become yellow and the red light to stay red. Putting these conditions in a decision table yields the table shown in Listing 7.1.

Listing 7.1 The first test for our controller

```
1  !|FirstLightSwitchingCrossingController                      |
2  |first light|second light|first light?|second light?|
3  |green      |red         |yellow      |red         |
```

When executing this test, FitNesse tells us that the class `FirstLightSwitch-ingCrossingController` is missing. Do you remember the package we put our glue code in? We will put the new classes into the same package.

We could add an import table to the crossing test as we did for the light state test. However, this would yield duplication of the package name, eventually leading future maintainers of the system to adapt to our decision now. In the end we could get a test suite where the package name for the glue code is spread all over the place. In order to avoid this maintenance nightmare, let's use a different approach for this test.

First, we create a new page under the `TrafficLight` suite called `SetUp`, permitting the default page type. We put the import table into the SetUp page and return to the test page for the light states. There is now a new collapsed section labeled SetUp. When we open it, we find out that our just-created setup page is included automatically by the framework. Let's remove the duplicated import statement from the test by hitting the edit button and removing it.

Now, we can execute the test for our crossing controller. It tells us that it's missing a class. We can implement the glue code by creating the class `FirstLightSwitchingCrossingController` in the package `org.trafficlights.test.acceptance`. After running the test with the empty class in place, FitNesse tells us that it tried to invoke two set functions and two query functions on that class—one setter and one query to verify the results for each light. We have to add these four functions to the class and re-execute the test. The resulting class is shown in Listing 7.2.

Listing 7.2 The first empty body for the controller glue code class

```
1 package org.trafficlights.test.acceptance;
2
3 import org.trafficlights.domain.LightState;
4
5 public class FirstLightSwitchingCrossingController {
6
7         public void setFirstLight(LightState state) {
8         }
9
10        public void setSecondLight(LightState state) {
11        }
12
13        public LightState firstLight() {
```

```
14                      return LightState.UNKNOWN;
15            }
16
17        public LightState secondLight() {
18                      return LightState.UNKNOWN;
19            }
20 }
```

We can now make the first test pass by returning the YELLOW state from the first light function and RED from the second light function. After making the changes and executing the FitNesse test, the first test passes, and we may check in these changes to the source code repository.

Now, as before, we may start to add more examples to the table. Since the table covers just switching the first light, we will start to iterate through the happy path cases where the second light is red, and the first light varies between the green, yellow, red and yellow, and red light. This results in the test examples as shown in Listing 7.3. They look similar to our specification table.

Listing 7.3 The basic happy path tests for the controller that switches the first light only

```
1 !|FirstLightSwitchingCrossingController                    |
2 |first light|second light|first light?|second light?|
3 |green       |red         |yellow      |red          |
4 |yellow      |red         |red         |red          |
5 |red, yellow|red         |green       |red          |
6 |red         |red         |red, yellow |red          |
```

When we run these examples, we notice that the second light does not need to change. In order to make this acceptance test pass, we can store the value of the first light in a local variable in our glue code and return the next state from the query firstLight (see Listing 7.4).

Listing 7.4 The body for the controller glue code class that actually switches the state

```
1 package org.trafficlights.test.acceptance;
2
3 import org.trafficlights.domain.LightState;
4
5 public class FirstLightSwitchingCrossingController {
6
```

```
7          LightState firstState;
8
9          public void setFirstLight(LightState state) {
10                  firstState = state;
11         }
12
13         public void setSecondLight(LightState state) {
14         }
15
16         public LightState firstLight() {
17                  return firstState.next();
18         }
19
20         public LightState secondLight() {
21                  return LightState.RED;
22         }
23 }
```

Rerunning the tests gives us a pass, and we should check these changes into the source code repository again.

The thing that worries me is that we have not used the second light state. So far, there is no need for it. For the invalid states, though, we will have to remember both states and turn the second light to a yellow blinking light if the end configuration of the two light states is invalid according to the law requirements.

Before starting this development, we should make some adaptations to the current code. Introducing the changes for the invalid configurations later will make our life easier after refactoring the current code. Let's take tiny steps while implementing the changes necessary for the validation of the two light states. First of all, I would like to store the second light state into a variable when the setter is invoked (see Listing 7.5).

Listing 7.5 The second light state is stored in a field

```
1 public class FirstLightSwitchingCrossingController {
2
3          LightState firstState;
4
5          LightState secondState;
6
7  ...
```

```
8
9          public void setSecondLight(LightState state) {
10                 secondState = state;
11         }
12  ...
13 }
```

All tests are still passing after this change.

The next thing we should change before tackling an invalid configuration is returning the previously stored second light state from the query method (see Listing 7.6).

Listing 7.6 The second light state is stored in a field

```
1 public class FirstLightSwitchingCrossingController {
2
3  ...
4          public LightState secondLight() {
5                  return secondState;
6          }
7
8 }
```

Tests are passing, check-in time.

Now, from the software design point of view, one thing is awkward. There are two setter methods and two queries. The query method for the second light state simply returns a previously stored value. That's exactly how a query method should behave. But the query method for the first light state returns a changed value. The query method certainly has a side effect when executed. It changes the state of the first light–although not physically right now, but we are working toward changing this.

The query method for the first method should just return a value that was previously calculated. This is called Command/Query-Separation.[1] But this leaves open the question of where I should change the state. In SLiM the execute() method of each fixture class is executed for a decision table after calling all setters. So, we should introduce an execute method to the FirstLightSwitchingController, which changes the state of the first light (see Listing 7.7).

---

1. http://pragprog.com/articles/tell-dont-ask

Listing 7.7 The first LightState is changed within the execute method

```
1 public class FirstLightSwitchingCrossingController {
2 ...
3         public LightState firstLight() {
4                 return firstState;
5         }
6
7 ...
8
9         public void execute() {
10                firstState = firstState.next();
11        }
12 }
```

Seeing all tests still passing, we know it's time for us to share this progress with our colleagues through the source repository.

At this point we can introduce the first test, which leads to an invalid combination. Let's take the first of the valid configurations and change the state of the second light in the second column. The resulting expected state should be the yellow blinking ones (see Listing 7.8).

Listing 7.8 The first invalid configuration

```
1 !|FirstLightSwitchingCrossingController                          |
2 |first light|second light|first light?|second light?|
3 |green       |red          |yellow       |red          |
4 |yellow      |red          |red          |red          |
5 |red, yellow|red          |green        |red          |
6 |red         |red          |red, yellow |red          |
7 |green       |red, yellow |yellow blink|yellow blink |
```

I would expect the controller to avoid invalid configurations before and after switching one of the lights. Therefore let's expect that the controller switches the traffic lights to a state in which car drivers become aware that something is wrong.

Since the validation logic is missing in the execute method, this new line in the table fails. In order to make this test pass, we have to check the two states for compatibility before switching the first state. The combination of a green light for one direction and a red and yellow light for another direction is invalid, since it would allow one direction to drive while the other direction expects to get green soon.

To the existing execute method of the glue code class we add a validation line that checks whether the first and second states should be shown together (see Listing 7.9).

Listing 7.9 A validation step is added to the controller before switching the light states

```
1 public class FirstLightSwitchingCrossingController {
2 ...
3         public void execute() {
4                 if (!LightState.RED.equals(secondState)) {
5                         firstState = LightState.UNKNOWN;
6                         secondState = LightState.UNKNOWN;
7                         return;
8                 }
9                 firstState = firstState.next();
10        }
11 }
```

In case the second light is not the red state, we get an invalid configuration and have to set both states to the invalid state: We indicate that there is something wrong. The return statement avoids any harm. We run the tests, see them all passing, but before we check in these changes, let's clean up the execute() method.

First of all, the condition in the if clause should get its own method so that we can extend it later in case we find more conditions for invalid configurations—and I'm quite certain we will. Let's extract a method to check for a proper light state configuration and call this method isValidLightStateConfiguration() (see Listing 7.10).

Listing 7.10 The validation method has been extracted from the if clause

```
1 public class FirstLightSwitchingCrossingController {
2 ...
3         public void execute() {
4                 if (!isValidLightStateConfiguration()) {
5                         firstState = LightState.UNKNOWN;
6                         secondState = LightState.UNKNOWN;
7                         return;
8                 }
9                 firstState = firstState.next();
10        }
```

```
11
12          private boolean isValidLightStateConfiguration() {
13                  return LightState.RED.equals(secondState);
14          }
15 }
```

After running all the tests, we can extract the code that sets both light states to the invalid configuration. We can achieve this by putting the two lines that set the first and second states to the unknown state into a method called warningConfiguration() (see Listing 7.11).

Listing 7.11 The setting of a warning configuration has been extracted from the if body

```
1 public class FirstLightSwitchingCrossingController {
2 ...
3          public void execute() {
4                  if (!isValidLightStateConfiguration()) {
5                          warningConfiguration();
6                          return;
7                  }
8                  firstState = firstState.next();
9          }
10
11          private boolean isValidLightStateConfiguration() {
12                  return LightState.RED.equals(secondState);
13          }
14
15          private void warningConfiguration() {
16                  firstState = LightState.UNKNOWN;
17                  secondState = LightState.UNKNOWN;
18          }
19 }
```

After running all the tests, I am confident to check in our changes.

Now, we can start extending the invalid examples by permutating the remaining states. Since the examples are various in number, we should put the invalid tests into their own table (see Listing 7.12). While adding one example after another, you should notice that all of them are passing.

Listing 7.12 All permutated invalid configurations put into their own table

```
 1  !2 Valid combinations
 2
 3  !|FirstLightSwitchingCrossingController                    |
 4  |first light|second light|first light?|second light?|
 5  |green        |red          |yellow        |red          |
 6  |yellow       |red          |red           |red          |
 7  |red, yellow|red          |green         |red          |
 8  |red          |red          |red, yellow |red          |
 9
10  !2 Invalid combinations
11
12  !|FirstLightSwitchingCrossingController                    |
13  |first light  |second light|first light?|second light?|
14  |green          |red, yellow |yellow blink|yellow blink |
15  |green          |green        |yellow blink|yellow blink |
16  |green          |yellow       |yellow blink|yellow blink |
17  |yellow         |red, yellow |yellow blink|yellow blink |
18  |yellow         |green        |yellow blink|yellow blink |
19  |yellow         |yellow       |yellow blink|yellow blink |
20  |red, yellow |red, yellow |yellow blink|yellow blink |
21  |red, yellow |green        |yellow blink|yellow blink |
22  |red, yellow |yellow       |yellow blink|yellow blink |
23  |red          |red, yellow |yellow blink|yellow blink |
24  |red          |green        |yellow blink|yellow blink |
25  |red          |yellow       |yellow blink|yellow blink |
26  |yellow blink|red          |yellow blink|yellow blink |
27  |yellow blink|red, yellow |yellow blink|yellow blink |
28  |yellow blink|green        |yellow blink|yellow blink |
29  |yellow blink|yellow       |yellow blink|yellow blink |
```

The combination that does not work correctly is the one with the yellow blinking first light and the red light. If we already have an invalid configuration in one direction, we can expect the other direction to switch to an invalid configuration, too. In order to achieve this we need to add a case in the glue code for the unknown light state (see Listing 7.13).

Listing 7.13 UNKNOWN light stats are now supported

```
1 public class FirstLightSwitchingCrossingController {
2 ...
3         private boolean isValidLightStateConfiguration() {
4                 return !LightState.UNKNOWN.equals(firstState)
      && LightState.RED.equals(secondState);
5           }
6
7 ...
8 }
```

Rerunning all the tests shows us that they are passing now. Let's check in the results immediately.

Refactoring

As before, we could declare our work finished and move on. But I start to get worried about the design of the code as well as the design of the examples. Let's see what we can do about this.

Refactoring the examples For the examples, the split between the happy path examples and the invalid examples led to high redundancy in the expected outcome of the invalid combinations. The expectation for the second table is the same all the time. Thus we can get rid of the two columns on the right altogether and express the intent of the test by saying that the following examples are invalid combinations (see Listing 7.14).

Listing 7.14 The scenario table to remove redundant information from the invalid combinations

```
1  ...
2  !2 Invalid combinations
3
4  !|scenario       |invalid combination|firstLight||secondLight|
5  |set first light |@firstLight                                 |
6  |set second light|@secondLight                                |
7  |execute                                                      |
8  |check           |first light        |yellow blink            |
9  |check           |second light       |yellow blink            |
10 ...
```

In this case, we can achieve this by extracting the common part to a scenario table. A scenario table is similar to a function in a programming language. In other frameworks this would have been an extraction of a keyword. The scenario table outlines the procedure for one function.

Reading the first table from the top indicates that our scenario is called invalid combination and takes two parameters, the firstLight and secondLight (see line 4). It then executes the following steps. First it sets the first light, then the second (starting at line 5), calls some execute method (line 7), and checks the results after switching the first light (starting at line 8). This should yield a configuration with blinking lights for the first and second traffic light.

Scenario tables are used within SLiM in combination with script tables. Therefore, we can take the name of the class that we used for our decision table earlier and declare it as a script table actor. The script table actor works similarly to the first line in a decision table. The only difference is that you may declare multiple script table actors on a test page, while you may only have one class for decision tables (see line 11 in Listing 7.15). The final table (see Listing 7.15) states all the combinations of invalid light configurations. Line 13 expresses that the just defined scenario invalid combination will be called multiple times. Line 14 indicates which column will be which parameter to the scenario. From line 15 forth all the different combinations are referenced.

Listing 7.15 Redundant information eliminated from the invalid combinations

```
1  ...
2  !2 Invalid combinations
3
4  !|scenario        |invalid combination|firstLight||secondLight|
5  |set first light |@firstLight                                |
6  |set second light|@secondLight                               |
7  |execute                                                     |
8  |check           |first light        |yellow blink          |
9  |check           |second light       |yellow blink          |
10
11 !|script|FirstLightSwitchingCrossingController|
12
13 !|invalid combination    |
14 |firstLight  |secondLight|
15 |green       |red, yellow|
16 |green       |green      |
17 |green       |yellow     |
```

```
18 |yellow        |red, yellow|
19 |yellow        |green      |
20 |yellow        |yellow     |
21 |red, yellow |red, yellow|
22 |red, yellow |green      |
23 |red, yellow |yellow     |
24 |red           |red, yellow|
25 |red           |green      |
26 |red           |yellow     |
27 |yellow blink|red        |
28 |yellow blink|red, yellow|
29 |yellow blink|green      |
30 |yellow blink|yellow     |
```

When we execute the tests, they all pass. The results now look a bit different than before. There is a collapsible section indicated by the arrow labeled "scenario" on each tested row of the invalid combination table. By clicking on it, it expands, and the result reveals each of the steps executed within the scenario (see Figure 7.1).

Scenario tables are automatically included from a page named after a convention similar to SetUp and TearDown pages. In order to make our test more condensed,

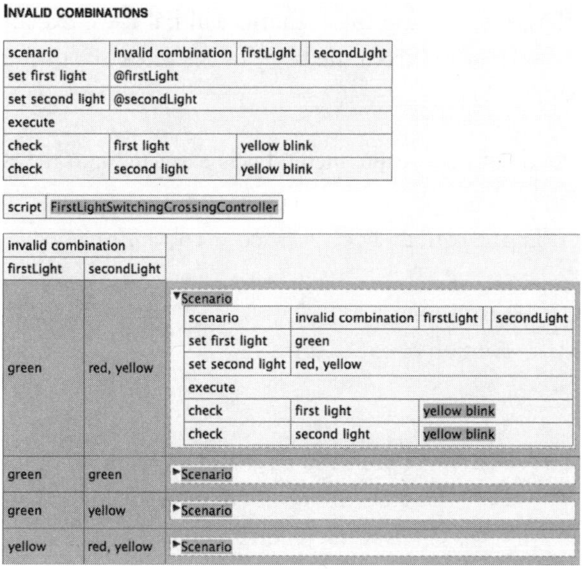

Figure 7.1 The scenario table results in a collapsible section

let's put the scenario definition into a page called `ScenarioLibrary` within the `CrossingControl` suite. After we rerun all of our tests after this extraction, we can check them in if they are still all passing.

There is one awkward thing in the scenario table as it stands right now. We directly reference the execute method. This makes reading the scenario table unnatural. We fix this by extracting a new public function from the execute body and using that instead. The name of the method should reveal its intent. Since our scenario table is the origin of our impression, we change the reference to `execute()` there first.

The question is what is a better way to express execute in this context? Oh, you suggest to call it "switch first light"? That's a great name. Since we deal with switching lights, it seems more natural to name a function `switchFirstLight()` in this context (see Listing 7.16).

Listing 7.16 The scenario table now references a more transparent operation

```
1 !|scenario          |invalid combination|firstLight||secondLight|
2 |set first light |@firstLight                                  |
3 |set second light|@secondLight                                 |
4 |switch first light                                            |
5 |check             |first light        |yellow blink          |
6 |check             |second light       |yellow blink          |
```

Of course, all the tests using the scenario will fail if we execute them. So, we quickly extract a new method from the body of the `execute()` method and make it public (see Listing 7.17).

Listing 7.17 The body of the execute method gets extracted into the switchFirstLight() method

```
1  public class FirstLightSwitchingCrossingController {
2  ...
3          public void execute() {
4                  switchFirstLight();
5          }
6
7          public void switchFirstLight() {
8                  if (!isValidLightStateConfiguration()) {
9                          warningConfiguration();
10                         return;
11                 }
```

```
12                    firstState = firstState.next();
13              }
14  ...
15  }
```

When running the tests, we see immediately that our changes are ready for check-in.

Refactoring the Glue Code   So far we implemented the solution directly in the glue code class rather than providing a domain class for it. The controller concept seems to be fine, but while doing the invalid configurations I got suspicious that there is another concept missing. Reviewing our tests, let's consider the concept of a light state validator that expresses what our domain model needs nicely. We want to validate whether the new light state configuration is going to be a valid combination of light states. Putting the responsibility into a validator sounds straightforward to me.

There are two other things I start worrying about. Our controller currently just handles two light states. In the future we may want to be able to switch between multiple directions—maybe left-turning vehicles get their own traffic lights for instance, or the three directions at a T-crossing are switched individually. Since we can assume that our controller will deal later with more directions, we should postpone any decision for more than one light state until we have to define examples for this case.

The other thing that came to my mind concerns what our controller does. The execute() method clearly just updates one of the light states. Maybe in the future there will be a need to switch more than one light at a time. To avoid premature optimization, let's leave the current design and functionality as is. In the future, when our examples drive such changes, we can still introduce them.

So, the only relevant change I see now is a validator for two light states. This time I see where my solution is heading. We are going to introduce a strategy object to validate state changes before calling next() on one of the possible directions.

As a designer, I feel safe using small refactoring steps on the code that we already have. For the new validator class, we will use the isValidLightState-Configuration() function as a basis (see Listing 7.18).

Listing 7.18 The function that we will refactor into its own class

```
1       private boolean isValidLightStateConfiguration() {
2               return !LightState.UNKNOWN.equals(firstState)
        && LightState.RED.equals(secondState);
3           }
```

We will be developing the validator class inside the glue code class and later move it to a package for production use. Before we do this, let's analyze the function. So far it depends on the two light states. Before extracting this to its own class, we will introduce the two states as a parameter to the function (see Listing 7.19).

Listing 7.19 The validation function after introducing two parameters

```
1  public class FirstLightSwitchingCrossingController {
2  ...
3        public void switchFirstLight() {
4               if (!isValidLightStateConfiguration(firstState,
       secondState)) {
5                      warningConfiguration();
6                      return;
7               }
8               firstState = firstState.next();
9        }
10
11       private boolean isValidLightStateConfiguration(
       LightState firstState, LightState secondState) {
12              return !LightState.UNKNOWN.equals(firstState)
       && LightState.RED.equals(secondState);
13       }
14 ...
15 }
```

After rerunning the tests in FitNesse, we gain the confidence that we didn't break anything by this movement.

Now we may refactor the isValidLightStateConfiguration(LightState, LightState) method into its own method object. In order to do this, we have to start with creating an empty validator class inside the CrossingController (see Listing 7.20).

Listing 7.20 The new empty validator class

```
1  public class FirstLightSwitchingCrossingController {
2  ...
3        private static class CrossingValidator {
4
5        }
6  }
```

Adding an empty class might not have broken anything, but to be sure about it, let's rerun the tests. Now, we can move the isValidLightStateConfiguration(LightState, LightState) function to our empty class. The refactoring function in our IDE doesn't provide us the choice to move the method to the CrossingValidator yet. In order to get this choice we have to introduce a new parameter–a CrossingValidator object (see Listing 7.21).

Listing 7.21   The validator is temporarily made a parameter to the validation function in order to move the method there

```
1  public class FirstLightSwitchingCrossingController {
2  ...
3          public void switchFirstLight() {
4                  if (!isValidLightStateConfiguration(new
      CrossingValidator(), firstState, secondState)) {
5                          warningConfiguration();
6                          return;
7                  }
8                  firstState = firstState.next();
9          }
10
11         private boolean isValidLightStateConfiguration(
      CrossingValidator validator, LightState firstState,
      LightState secondState) {
12                 return !LightState.UNKNOWN.equals(firstState)
      && LightState.RED.equals(secondState);
13         }
14  ...
15 }
```

Since this might have broken something in the refactoring, we rerun the tests to feel safe. Now, the IDE offers suggestions to move the isValidLightStateConfiguration(LightState, LightState) function to our new CrossingValidator class. You can see the result in Listing 7.22.

Listing 7.22   The validator after moving the validation function there

```
1  public class FirstLightSwitchingCrossingController {
2  ...
3          public void switchFirstLight() {
```

```
4                    if (!new CrossingValidator().
       isValidLightStateConfiguration(firstState, secondState)) {
5                            warningConfiguration();
6                            return;
7                    }
8                    firstState = firstState.next();
9             }
10
11  ...
12        static class CrossingValidator {
13
14                boolean isValidLightStateConfiguration(
       LightState firstState, LightState secondState) {
15                        return !LightState.UNKNOWN.equals(
       firstState) && LightState.RED.equals(secondState);
16                }
17
18        }
19  }
```

You're right, we have to re-execute the tests to see that this step didn't break anything. Green, OK. Let's go on and clean up our code now. The new CrossingValidator() inside the if-clause bothers me. Let's create a field to hold the validator and initialize it with the new validator by first extracting a local variable from the constructor call, and then turning that new variable into a field (see Listing 7.23).

Listing 7.23 The validator is turned into a field within the controller class

```
1  public class FirstLightSwitchingCrossingController {
2
3        private CrossingValidator validator = new
       CrossingValidator();
4  ...
5        public void switchFirstLight() {
6                if (!validator.isValidLightStateConfiguration(
       firstState, secondState)) {
7                        warningConfiguration();
8                        return;
9                }
```

```
10                    firstState = firstState.next();
11           }
12  ...
13  }
```

Rerunning the tests gains me the confidence that we didn't break anything. At this point we are nearly ready to turn the new validator class into its own top-level class. But before doing this I would like to rename the method `isValid-LightStateConfiguration()` into something shorter. Method names should get shorter the more public the method is [Mar08a]. Thus far we have dealt with a protected function inside an inner class, so the length was quite right. But if we turn this now into a public method, we want to rename it before doing so. The new name that comes to mind that still expresses the intent is `isValidConfiguration()`, and we should rename the function to this new name. After that we can add the public modifiers to both the inner class as well as the method itself. While at it, we also drop the static modifier from the class declaration (see Listing 7.24).

Listing 7.24 The validator method after the rename

```
1    public class CrossingValidator {
2
3            public boolean isValidConfiguration(LightState
        firstState, LightState secondState) {
4                    return !LightState.UNKNOWN.equals(
        firstState) && LightState.RED.equals(secondState);
5            }
6
7        }
```

Rerunning the tests tells us that the code still works flawlessly. Now we can ask the IDE to extract a top-level class from this inner class and move it into the domain package. Oh, sure, we have to execute the FitNesse tests as well. If they reveal no problem, we are fine with our changes.

Before we check in these changes, there is a problem. So far, all the classes in the domain package have their own unit tests in place as well as some tests in the acceptance test suite. But our new `CrossingValidator` is the first class without unit tests in the domain package. This could end in unhappy surprises for the developer who makes some adaptations and doesn't or cannot run all of the acceptance tests—maybe when the acceptance test suite has grown a lot in both size and execution time. Since we are responsible for communicating what this class does, and we remember it right now, let's retrofit some unit tests to the newly created class. As before, we find that JUnit's parameterized tests express this in the most elegant way (see Listing 7.25).

Listing 7.25 The retrofitted unit tests for our validator class

```
 1 package org.trafficlights.domain;
 2
 3 import static java.util.Arrays.*;
 4 import static org.junit.Assert.*;
 5 import static org.trafficlights.domain.LightState.*;
 6
 7 import java.util.List;
 8
 9 import org.junit.Test;
10 import org.junit.runner.RunWith;
11 import org.junit.runners.Parameterized;
12 import org.junit.runners.Parameterized.Parameters;
13
14 @RunWith(Parameterized.class)
15 public class CrossingValidatorTest {
16
17         @Parameters
18         public static List<Object[]> values() {
19                 return asList(new Object[][] {
20                                     {RED, RED, true},
21                                     {GREEN, RED, true},
22                                     {YELLOW, RED, true},
23                                     {RED_YELLOW, RED, true},
24                                     {UNKNOWN, RED, false},
25                                     {GREEN, GREEN, false},
26                                     {YELLOW, GREEN, false},
27                                     {RED_YELLOW, GREEN, false},
28                                     {RED, GREEN, true},
29                         });
30         }
31
32         private LightState firstState;
33         private LightState secondState;
```

```
34          private boolean valid;
35
36          public CrossingValidatorTest(LightState firstState,
       LightState secondState,
37                              boolean valid) {
38                  this.firstState = firstState;
39                  this.secondState = secondState;
40                  this.valid = valid;
41          }
42
43          @Test
44          public void isValidConfiguration() {
45                  assertEquals(valid, new CrossingValidator().
       isValidConfiguration(firstState, secondState));
46          }
47 }
```

While retrofitting the unit tests, I notice a flaw in our design. The light state with RED as first light and GREEN as second light is valid, but our validator rejects it as invalid. This is surely going to bother us in the future when either of us forget about the particular implementation details. So, it's a good thing that we started to develop those unit tests, and it shows the difference between our acceptance tests—which passed the requirements—and our unit tests—which revealed the problem in the design.

The problem originates from the fact that our controller does one validation for the light state configuration before switching the first state and after the switch in one function. But as we construct the validator, it checks the condition before the switch as well as after the speculated switch and delivers a result for both states.

This analysis leaves us with two options. Either we split up the validation into a pre-switch and post-switch validation, and make the change only if we get a valid configuration, or we leave the validator as is, but rename it to reflect this.

The disadvantage of the second approach would be that too much knowledge is put into the validator class. It would be a very specialized validator for a limited use—switching the first light. Also the validator would know too much about its use. As a designer, this does not seem right to me.

The first approach comes with the advantage that the validator's purpose is clear. This advantage outweighs to me the double validation step. Therefore, let's change the design of the controller. The first step in changing the design is to revisit the function that switches the first light. After switching the first light, we add a second validation step to the function, which should not break the existing behavior (see Listing 7.26).

Listing 7.26 We added a second validation after the light was switched

```
 1 public class FirstLightSwitchingCrossingController {
 2 ...
 3        public void switchFirstLight() {
 4                if (!validator.isValidConfiguration(firstState
      , secondState)) {
 5                        warningConfiguration();
 6                        return;
 7                }
 8                firstState = firstState.next();
 9
10                if (!validator.isValidConfiguration(firstState
      , secondState)) {
11                        warningConfiguration();
12                }
13         }
14 ...
15 }
```

Rerunning the acceptance tests shows that we did not break anything. Now, we may take care of the flawed validator, and our last unit test. The test for the combination of a red and a green light failed. This implies a missing condition in the validate function of our validator. Let's add this (see Listing 7.27).

Listing 7.27 The corrected validation function

```
 1 public class CrossingValidator {
 2
 3        public boolean isValidConfiguration(LightState
      firstState, LightState secondState) {
 4                if (LightState.UNKNOWN.equals(firstState))
      return false;
 5                if (LightState.RED.equals(secondState)) return
       true;
 6                if (LightState.RED.equals(firstState) &&
      LightState.GREEN.equals(secondState)) return true;
```

```
 7                      return false;
 8              }
 9
10 }
```

The code now passes the tests. At this point we can extend the unit tests further. Let's continue to permutate the states. When we get to the combination of RED and RED_YELLOW, we hit the next failing test (see Listing 7.28).

Listing 7.28 The tests up to the point where we hit another failing configuration

```
 1 @RunWith(Parameterized.class)
 2 public class CrossingValidatorTest {
 3
 4         @Parameters
 5         public static List<Object[]> values() {
 6                 return asList(new Object[][] {
 7                                 {RED, RED, true},
 8                                 {GREEN, RED, true},
 9                                 {YELLOW, RED, true},
10                                 {RED_YELLOW, RED, true},
11                                 {UNKNOWN, RED, false},
12                                 {GREEN, GREEN, false},
13                                 {YELLOW, GREEN, false},
14                                 {RED_YELLOW, GREEN, false},
15                                 {RED, GREEN, true},
16                                 {UNKNOWN, GREEN, false},
17                                 {GREEN, RED_YELLOW, false},
18                                 {YELLOW, RED_YELLOW, false},
19                                 {RED, RED_YELLOW, true},
20                         });
21         }
22 ..
23 }
```

At this point we can extend the previous special condition. Since we are sure on the third line of the isValidConfiguration(LightState, LightState) method that the second light cannot be RED, we can remove the second part of that condition (see Listing 7.29).

Listing 7.29 The adapted validation function

```
1 public class CrossingValidator {
2
3       public boolean isValidConfiguration(LightState
    firstState, LightState secondState) {
4               if (LightState.UNKNOWN.equals(firstState))
    return false;
5               if (LightState.RED.equals(secondState)) return
        true;
6               if (LightState.RED.equals(firstState)) return
        true;
7               return false;
8           }
9
10 }
```

This code passes the tests, and we may continue adding more configurations to our parameterized test. The next failing test in my permutations is the combination of RED and UNKNOWN. A quick look into the validation function shows that we may resolve this by catching the blinking light condition as the second light (see Listing 7.30).

Listing 7.30 The validation function after adding the check for the second light to be blinking

```
1 public class CrossingValidator {
2
3       public boolean isValidConfiguration(LightState
    firstState, LightState secondState) {
4               if (LightState.UNKNOWN.equals(firstState) ||
    LightState.UNKNOWN.equals(secondState)) return false;
5               if (LightState.RED.equals(secondState)) return
        true;
6               if (LightState.RED.equals(firstState)) return
        true;
7               return false;
8           }
9
10 }
```

After seeing that this code passes the test, let's finish the remaining permutations (see Listing 7.31). Without further failing tests, the code passes all the tests. Sure, let's execute all the existing acceptance tests as well. They are all passing, so let's check in our redesign into the repository.

Listing 7.31 The final unit tests for the validator

```
1  @RunWith(Parameterized.class)
2  public class CrossingValidatorTest {
3
4          @Parameters
5          public static List<Object[]> values() {
6                  return asList(new Object[][] {
7                                  {RED, RED, true},
8                                  {GREEN, RED, true},
9                                  {YELLOW, RED, true},
10                                 {RED_YELLOW, RED, true},
11                                 {UNKNOWN, RED, false},
12                                 {GREEN, GREEN, false},
13                                 {YELLOW, GREEN, false},
14                                 {RED_YELLOW, GREEN, false},
15                                 {RED, GREEN, true},
16                                 {UNKNOWN, GREEN, false},
17                                 {GREEN, RED_YELLOW, false},
18                                 {YELLOW, RED_YELLOW, false},
19                                 {RED, RED_YELLOW, true},
20                                 {RED_YELLOW, RED_YELLOW, false},
21                                 {UNKNOWN, RED_YELLOW, false},
22                                 {GREEN, YELLOW, false},
23                                 {YELLOW, YELLOW, false},
24                                 {RED, YELLOW, true},
25                                 {RED_YELLOW, YELLOW, false},
26                                 {UNKNOWN, YELLOW, false},
27                                 {GREEN, UNKNOWN, false},
28                                 {YELLOW, UNKNOWN, false},
29                                 {RED, UNKNOWN, false},
30                                 {RED_YELLOW, UNKNOWN, false},
31                                 {UNKNOWN, UNKNOWN, false}
32                  });
```

```
33              }
34  . . .
35  }
```

And after this lesson, we both are surely going to add unit tests for our design early on the next time.

Summary

Let's take a break. While doing so we should reflect over the past few minutes. We added a first crossing with two intersecting roads. We started to work our way from the light state and its changes to the controller, which has the responsibility for coordinating state changes between the two different directions, and preventing two opposing directions from showing the green light at the same time.

Example by example we first built everything into the glue code. After getting the acceptance tests to pass, we put on our designer hats and let our knowledge from implementing the glue code guide our next actions. This time we decided to refactor the code we had into a new concept within our design. While retrofitting unit tests to the code, we found out that we created a flawed design and changed the underlying design to express the intent more meaningfully. As a take-away, we found out that acceptance tests alone are not enough to guide our design. This is the main difference between TDD, which guides the design, and ATDD, which guides the requirements. TDD focuses on tiny unit tests. It thereby helps to move the design of the classes in a certain direction. ATDD, on the other hand, focuses on the requirements, the specification of the functionality. TDD deals with technical implementations; ATDD deals with acceptance criteria from a business perspective.

On the technology level, we saw decision tables used again, but also learned about scenario tables used similarly as decision tables. We could have transformed the successful tests for switching the first light as well and gotten rid of the last column merely mentioning the red state of the second light. We explicitly decided against this step, because this might obscure the outcome for the successful state changes for the test reader in the future. For the invalid state changes, the outcome is completely the same all the time. The decision to hide the repeated yellow blinking states was well put into the scenario table at this point. One additional reason to hide the yellow blink combination is that we now can change the representation of the invalid configuration in a single place for all tests that might be implemented in the future as well—as long as that scenario can be used.

Chapter 8
Discover and Explore

In this part we have seen how a traffic light system evolves. We worked from the outside into our application. One of the main differences from the first part is that we used the glue code to motivate the design for our domain classes. Another thing that enabled us to work in this way is that the designer of the system is the same person—or better, pair—as the one writing the glue code.

In fact, while implementing the glue code for the test automation, we noticed possible designs for the production class. In the first case we decided to implement a state pattern once we could see how the glue code differentiates the light states. In the second case we could extract the light switching controller directly from the glue class.

One thing that we realized too late was the need for unit tests for our glue code. Due to the lack of driving the code through unit tests, we ran into the problem with multiple responsibilities in the controller code when we extracted the code and put it under test. If we had done this step earlier, we could have realized the multiple responsibilities in the code sooner by reviewing the tests. Another take-away here was that we should strive for adding unit tests for our support code as early as possible. With tests in place, we might have found out about the multiple responsibilities way sooner, before heading for the extraction.

The ATDD approach makes use of test automation. Since test automation is software development, it makes sense to implement the test automation code using TDD whenever possible. You might be able to get started with functional tests from a business perspective rather quickly. But as you pile up more and more glue code, you will also become less and less aware of side effects to changes in that code. With proper unit tests even for your glue code in place, you can avoid that trap.

So, with ATDD you may also drive the production code as well as discover and explore the domain. But keep yourself aware that you had better add unit tests to your code soon enough before painting yourself into the corner. As a wrap-up, we will take a closer look at these more technical characteristics of the ATDD approach.

Discover the Domain

In this part we used the specifications to discover the domain of the underlying system. Initially, we had a vague idea of the underlying structure for the production code. While automating one example after another, we validated our thoughts. When we had a clear idea about how the production design might look, we started to write the production class for the domain code.

The implementation of the glue code helped to discover the domain. Once we could spot an implementation that supported the examples identified thus far, we could reflect on the code and try to find patterns that motivate the code for the domain. Once we could see the domain behavior growing in the glue code, the step toward either extracting the domain code from the glue code or writing it in parallel in a new class became obvious.

For the light state transitions, we discovered the need for a controller to control more than one light and coordinate state transitions between lights. The discovery of the controller gave the implementation new momentum. As we could see where we were heading, we extracted the domain code from the glue code. We noticed that we had forgotten a validator for different light state combinations. This discovery helped to improve the code even further.

For the evolution of the state concept to represent a light state, we developed the code in parallel to the existing glue code. We drove the design of the different light states based upon our previous experiences. In order to drive the design, we used test-driven development with microtests for the different states and transitions. Once we had finished the state pattern, we were able to replace the existing logic in the glue code with our new state enumeration and validate our new domain object against the already existing acceptance tests.

One of the problems with the latter approach to ATDD is that we could have found out way too late through a wrong implementation. If we had hooked up the new domain object in the glue code and had seen many errors in the acceptance tests, we would have needed to take a large step back to a clean basis. Such big steps are risky in terms of code design.

Because of this, I usually try to wait one passing acceptance longer to see the resulting design more clearly before taking such a large step. In case of the light state enumeration, I proposed waiting a bit longer than I would have when developing the code using TDD. In general, I know that I can rely on some of my expertise, but when it comes to acceptance tests, I try to withhold this thought and move one step closer toward the emerging design. This is a trade-off decision. While the design of the glue code might start to degenerate quickly if I wait too long, I also know that I might end up with an even worse design for my production code if I push for the refactoring too early.

Larger refactorings are not a big problem because today's IDEs support small- and large-scale refactorings in the code base quite well. So, the longer I can play around with different options for my domain code, the better my decision will be regarding the resulting production code.

Another point is crucial when working on a team of more than one pair of programmers. You want others to see what you do early. Continuous Integration (CI) [DMG07] of tiny little changes help to avoid the merging hell. With tiny adaptations you can oversee side effects while merging. If you extend the batch size of the changes, you might find yourself in the situation where you need to merge one month of code in several separate branches. I once heard from a company where this took two weeks. Usually I check in my results very often, several times per day.

Drive the Production Code

Starting with the examples first manifests a specification for the software. You can directly validate whether your software fulfills the specification by automating it. This is why Gojko Adzic proposed to rename Acceptance Test-driven Development to Specification by Example [Adz09, Adz11].

In the first part we saw how programmers and testers can work in parallel using the ATDD approach. In this part we paired together on some tests. Working from the example to the production code drives the design of the domain. Instead of working in parallel, we started with the examples. By automating the examples, we not only discovered the domain, but also drove the implementation of the production code.

The advantage here lies in the fact that every relevant line of production code will have automated acceptance tests when applying ATDD in this manner. The architecture of your production system will be testable by definition, and it will be covered to a large degree by automated tests.

Another advantage is the fact that you covered actual requirements with your automated tests. Despite checking for irrelevant conditions, the examples express what the domain experts really care about.

The high degree of coverage for your production code provides you with valuable feedback when moving to the next iteration. In 2008 I started to play around with the FitNesse code base. Since it's an open source system, I could download the source code and see what it does. At first, I played a bit with the code, trying to add a new functionality or two. Later I fixed bugs in the system. There were roughly 2000 unit tests in place alongside 200 acceptance tests. These tests ran all together in less than five minutes. The test suite provided me with feedback within the next five minutes whenever I broke something. This not only helped me learn about the code base, but it also helped me notice side effects to my changes.

A good functional test suite can help introduce new colleagues to a system as I was able to introduce myself to the FitNesse code base. Through short execution times and quick feedback your colleagues will also be able to work with your code base. You can easily achieve collective code and test ownership with this background. In such a system everyone feels safe changing anything without the excuses that I can't do any changes in the code or tests since it's another person's portion of the code or test base.

When your software needs extensions or maintenance, you will also revisit your examples. Since the examples in your automated acceptance tests tell the story of the project so far, you have a documentation system in place. Because the tests are executable and tell you by the press of a button whether your product fulfills the specification, you created an executable specification for your product. This also means that the specification should be kept up to date. These benefits all derive naturally when you drive your code base with the examples.

Test Your Glue Code

One of the immediate lessons for me after we failed dramatically with the extraction of the validator is to test my glue code. Just after extracting the behavior and retrofitting unit tests to the production code, we could realize that our initial design was flawed. We could have prevented that by test-driving our glue code right from the start.

On second thought, this is probably context-free advice. I often find myself exploring the domain of the production system. During exploration mode I come up with questions about the domain so quickly that I leave out unit tests to my code. In exploration mode I try to find out more about the domain itself. When I feel comfortable with my understanding of the domain, I fall back to the code base before I went into exploration mode and start over using TDD. I do this consciously in order to let my thoughts wander. I start interviewing the problem domain in code and try to reach a better understanding of the problem in exploration mode. During this thinking mode, I find my brain in a similar state as during brainstorming. My right hemisphere is highly engaged, coming up with rich thoughts. If I break this stream of thoughts and ideas, I risk losing momentum.

Unfortunately, this often comes back at me. Once I run out of new ideas, I find myself with code that is hard to test. When I find myself in such a mess, I know that it's time to throw away what I have produced so far and start over from scratch. This might sound painful, to throw away your code that looks so beautiful in the editor, but it's not the code that should last as an end result, rather the thinking and learning that you have put into it. If I start over now, I know that I will end up with a more flexible design and can even drive the known steps with unit tests right from the start.

In general, testing my glue code can happen in two different ways. In the first case, my glue code is straightforward, contains no structuring elements like if and loops, and each function contains no more than ten lines. This code is easy to understand. It's short so that a reader of the code can grasp in an instant what it's about. When I extract functions from my glue code, I keep an eye on the method names and give them intent-revealing names. With such simple code I don't have any worries that I find myself unable to understand it in a year from now. In order to test this simple code, I am happy if I execute my acceptance tests and see them passing. Executing the acceptance tests in order to test my glue code is fine in this case.

The second case of glue code consists of branches and loops. Even here, methods and functions are no longer than ten lines, but the conditional logic gives me a headache at times. I know that I will be lost in a year from now if I let this code stand on its own. In this case I know it's time for me to get my hands dirty by writing unit tests for this code. This helps the reader of the code to understand my thought process and to make extensions to the code if necessary. Just executing the acceptance tests is not enough in this case because I would have to execute many of them to cover all the conditional outcomes.

As a general rule, whenever I end up with a conditional statement in my glue code, I think hard how to unit test this piece. At one company I discovered the need for an interface for service calls toward an EJB system. I could easily mock that interface for the unit tests of my glue code. With guidance from *Growing Object-oriented Software, Guided by Tests* [FP09] I created a fluent API to test and mock the remote calls to the system under test for fast unit tests. Since this was a well-known API for me, I could easily grow tests for this glue code with high statement coverage (above 90%). When executing the tests in the test framework against the real system, I could replace the service executor with one that used reflection to fetch the proper local and remote home for the EJB service. The ServiceExecutor became a needle eye for calls to the other system that I could conveniently replace for my unit tests.

Since every single call to the remote service goes through a single point, I called this approach the Needle Eye pattern. Calls to an external system became a needle eye. This means that there are either some restrictions to this subsystem or there is some convention in place. In our case, the package names of the EJB2 services followed a strict naming convention. This allowed us to use reflection in order to find the local and remote home for a given service input. We encapsulated the calls to the remote system in a simple interface that provided an execute method for a common service input class and returned the output from that service (see Listing 8.1).

Listing 8.1 Signature of the EJB2 service executor for the Needle Eye pattern

```
1 public Output execute(Input serviceInput);
```

For our fixture classes, we used dependency injection in the constructor to replace the concrete service executor that used reflection to locate the real service home with a mocked one that the unit test would prepare with proper expectations. From this point we could also simulate thrown exceptions from the system under test, thereby achieving a high statement coverage of the unit tests for our glue code. This gave us great confidence in our test code while the project evolved.

Value Your Glue Code

In general, I treat my test code at least as well as my production code. Usually I value my glue code even higher than I value my production code because my glue code sits between two vital points in my development project.

The production code, on one hand, could be changed in every single iteration. Changes to an existing feature may happen nearly every time. That makes the code that talks directly to the application under test quite unstable. In *Agile Software Development–Patterns, Principles, and Practices* [Mar02], Robert Martin refers to the Stable Dependencies Principle. Packages in the code should depend on more stable packages. Since the code near to the unstable code of the application is unstable as well, it makes sense to encapsulate changes to this part of the code and make it depend upon more stable structures in the code base. Usually I achieve this with either a wrapper or an implementation of the delegation pattern (see [GHJV94]).

The second consideration for my glue code consists of the instability in the test language. Your test data form a language that represents the domain for your application. As development on the application proceeds, your test data also evolve. This means that the glue code that connects the test data with the application under test also needs to evolve. As our understanding of the underlying concepts change, my glue code needs to have the flexibility to change as well.

Usually I put behaviors that change alongside the development of the test language in their own classes. This involves for example concepts like money (a floating point number with a currency symbol), durations, or time. Another solution to this problem sometimes is to use an enumeration in the production code and provide the necessary conversion with an editor like we saw it in this part with the light state enum. The main advantage of this approach is that I can provide a conversion method easily. Sometimes I find out that I needed that concept in the domain anyway. At this point I am usually glad that I already have the conversion mechanism from my glue code as a by-product.

Between these two unstable interfaces lies some tiny layer of code that interconnects the two domain representations with each other. The smaller I can keep this layer, the better designed my domain classes usually are. When I find I need a lot more code to connect production concepts with acceptance test concepts, I reflect on my current design. More often than not I find my domain object lacking a basic concept. By extracting that concept from the glue code to my domain code, I keep my glue code as simple as possible—but no simpler than that.

Putting it all together, we have highly unstable dependencies toward the production system and toward the test data. There should be a thin line connecting the two worlds with each other. If this is not the case, take a larger view of your production, support, and glue code and see if you can improve anything there. If you don't see an opportunity to do so, continue to grow new tests, but keep an eye on this particular code. Over time your understanding of the domain may change, and you will see new opportunities for this portion in your code.

Summary

The "driven" part of ATDD puts emphasize on how to drive your whole application from the outside in. In this part we saw how acceptance tests help you to discover the domain of your application.

Discovering the domain alone is not enough. We also needed to drive our production code from the acceptance tests. Working from the acceptance tests inwards towards the system enabled us to see crucial design decisions for our production classes. In the long run this will help us a lot.

We also learned that we should value the code that we write to test our systems. One major reason I see test automation approaches failing at clients, is that they don't value their test code. Test automation is software development. That means we have to refactor it and align to the same principles as our production code. I found the Single Responsibility Principle, the Open-Closed Principle, the Interface Segregation Principle, and the Dependency Inversion Principle especially helpful for designing my glue code.

One side effect from such principles is that we should test our glue code. By that I mean not to execute it through the acceptance tests, but to really use unit tests to drive your glue code. Whenever possible divide your glue code to smaller functions that you can test easily in separation. Even if this is impossible for you, you should strive to find ways as the Needle Eye pattern to decouple the system under test from your glue code. Otherwise a small change to the system can cause a large change to your safety-net of acceptance test. Don't go there.

Part III

Principles of Acceptance Test-Driven Development

In this part we will take a closer look on the principles behind what we have seen. Why does Specification by Example work? Which problems should we watch out for? And are there any patterns behind this approach?

Chapter 9
Use Examples

In the first two parts of this book, the actual work started with examples derived from the business goals. For good examples, you need to have domain knowledge—or at least an easy access to someone who has. In the first example, the team did not have enough domain knowledge—and they received that feedback from their earlier failings. The team at Major International Airport Corp. therefore sat together in a workshop. To compensate for their lack of domain knowledge, they invited business expert Bill to join them. Together with Bill's help, Phyllis and Tony were able to derive examples for the business rules regarding airport parking lot costs.

In the second example, we worked together through a problem where I felt I had enough domain knowledge. We could have found ourselves trapped until it was too late. For the depth that we covered with this example, we had sufficient domain knowledge, so we could start after organizing some of our thoughts.

Examples are the first pillar in working with acceptance test-driven development, specification by example, behavior-driven development, or whatever you might call it. You can always work with examples of any kind, regardless of whether you automate the examples later.

Once I applied this approach in a company that was doing product development using a derivation of waterfall development. I was working in the System Integration department. The system we were integrating was a mobile phone rating and billing solution. We configured that system for use by the end customer while the Product Development department developed the product for a larger customer base. The product was highly configurable for different tariffs in the domain of mobile phones. One day our product development came up with a redesign of the GUIs used to configure the product. Unfortunately, a feature from an earlier release dealing with different workflows and approvals for new tariffs had become an obstruction. Since we were the customer and domain experts on configuring the product, the colleagues from product development reached out to us.

We held three meetings to clarify the problem and come up with a redesign that would benefit both departments. Previously, the system had a workflow for bringing in new tariffs into the system. The old workflow never worked for a real customer. When the product should support modular pieces for the single configuration file up to that point, this old workflow would have made things worse. The configuration component would have needed to support the validation of multiple working sets and to validate changes and dependencies across multiple working sets. This would eventually end in a mess for the product's testing department as well.

Within a three-hour workshop we discussed the whole workflow. With the vision of the new solution in mind, we came up with examples describing the future workflow with the split-up configuration. When the updated version arrived six months later, everyone was happy with it.

The examples we identified in the workshop were very high level. The testing department at that time did not have the abilities to automate these tests at the level we discussed them. The conversation about the requirements alone led to a better implementation of the product and a better customer experience on our side.

Regardless of whether you automate your examples, there are some things to watch out for. This chapter is about these things to watch for while using examples. The key factors that influence the success of your approach are the format the examples are written in, how detailed the examples are, and whether you considered any gaps in your overall approach.

Use a Proper Format

Expressing your tests using examples raises the question of how to express these examples. Although you might think that expressing examples is pretty easy, some patterns emerged during the past decade within teams applying ATDD.

The proper format for you depends on factors in your team, your project, and your organization. First of all, you need to consider who is going to read the tests after you created them. This probably includes yourself, the programmer who is going to develop the feature described by the examples, and your product owner or customer. You may also consider a future test maintainer if you hand over your tests to a different team or department or even company. All these future test readers may want to get a quick picture of the feature that you describe today. That's where a common way to express your examples becomes relevant.

Keeping all these possible target groups in mind, you should strive for examples that can be understood by any of these people. This means that you shouldn't bother writing technical descriptions of the workflow unless all people involved can make meaning out of them. We could have written the examples for our traffic light controller in the following way:

> If the green signal circuit for direction A and direction B are turned on, shut down the traffic light controller to a failsafe state. In the failsafe state, the yellow lights will be blinking constantly. Only a technician is allowed to bring the traffic lights out of this failsafe state after inspecting it. The controller has to log all state changes for the technical analysis in such cases.

This is a more narrative style such as you might find in a traditional specification. Now, reconsider the way we wrote down our examples. The first thing you might notice is that we didn't bother with the logging requirement at all—maybe this will be part of some future development. But we also noted all the circumstances when the failsafe mode shall be enabled. This more declarative style to write down examples provides a lot more information in the future when we have to read and extend the examples. And this information will also serve as communication device for real customers—and even users of the system such as you and me.

ATDD-friendly test automation frameworks split up test data and test automation code necessary for executing the tests. Since the test automation code glues together the development of your tests and the development of your application, I deliberately also call it glue code. The glue code may be implemented in different languages within the different available tools. Most tools are built upon some convention for calling functions in the glue code. With the splitting of the test data from the glue code, you can define the test examples independently of any particular implementation of the application.

There are many ways to write down examples for your application requirements. The most popular approach in the past few years is the one from behavior-driven development (BDD). The BDD format emerges around the terms Given-When-Then, which help to structure the expectations of a particular feature.

Another popular way to express examples is tabulated formats. There are some variations, but all have in common three different formats: one form of input-output mapping, one form of queries, and one form of actions as in workflows.

A third way to express examples are keywords or data-driven tests. With keywords you can combine different levels of abstraction in your test language. You can decide to use lower-level functions for tests focused on lower levels of your application, but you can also combine lower level functions to yield a higher level of abstraction. With keywords, these different levels of abstraction become fluent in your test description thereby forming a language for your domain in your tests.

Behavior-Driven Development

BDD was first described by Dan North [Nor06]. North mentioned the Given-When-Then paradigm in this article for the first time. While BDD consists of more than using Given-When-Then as a method to express the behavior of the features, this particular syntax has become almost a synonym for BDD in the past years. We saw the Given-When-Then format in the airport example. The three steps in the BDD format are arranged around the keywords Given, When, and Then. As an example, consider Listing 9.1, which searches Google for the term ATDD and expects to find lots of results.

Listing 9.1 A basic search on the Internet

```
1 Feature: Google Search
2   As an Internet user I want to use Google for searches
3
4   Scenario: Search for ATDD
5     Given the default Google page
6     When I search for 'ATDD'
7     Then I will find lots of results
```

In the Given part you express all preconditions for the particular behavior. The preconditions form the context for the description of the behavior. This includes any particular settings in an expressive manner. In the example above line 5 ensures the precondition that I have a browser open and that it has opened the default Google page. In the airport example we didn't have any givens, since all tests were based upon the parking lot calculator being open in a browser window. There was no reason to deviate from this default. In general, you want to express in the Given part anything that differs from a default case. For a system with different types of accounts, you will express which account you are working on in this particular example. For a system of various web pages, you may want to express the particular page where your example is operated. For a workflow in an application, you may want to express all the data that is relevant and that you expect to have been entered in the previous steps of the workflow, right before beginning the operation on the described part of the workflow. There may be more than one Given part, they are usually combined through consecutive And statements.

In the When part, you describe the operation and all the parameters that you are triggering. In the example above, we express in line 6 that we would like to search for a specific term. The operation that we want to trigger is basically entering some text in a textfield on a web page and hitting the default button. Other examples might be that you want to express that you reloaded an account with some money, that you entered different values to a web page form, or that you proceeded to the checkout of an online shop after filling your cart. The When part should describe something that happens [dFAdF10]. This may be a particular trigger from a user, an event outside the current subsystem, such as asynchronous messages from a third-party Internet service or a function within the computer system like a time-out. Additionally, there should be exactly one action step in any scenario description. This gives the described scenario a small enough focus.

The Then part describes post-conditions after executing the action from the When part. In most cases these are assertions against the system. In the example on Google search, we check in line 7 that there are lots of search results. As another example after reloading an account with some amount, you can check the bonus amount that your system shall provide. For a web page form, such as the parking lot calculator, you can assert calculated parking costs based on your own expectations. Like Given statements, several Then statements may be chained by using And as connector.

One of the mantras in behavior-driven development is outside-in development. BDD favors the development of code based upon requirements from the customer. The purpose of the workshop in the airport parking lot example was to derive the scope for the calculator based upon the business goals. The team achieved this by expressing the requirements without spoiling the implementation of the code by a predefined solution. The purpose of the requirements elicitation is to explore the space of possible solutions [GW89], which means to explore any solutions that fulfill the business rules. During the design process the designer seeks the best trade-off between possible solution parameters. The team at Major International Airport Corp. achieved this by abstracting the examples they identified without having a particular implementation of the user interface in mind. In fact, the examples can be hooked up to a new user interface by replacing the step definitions with definitions for the new user interface. Since the business rules probably will not change when using a different user interface, examples that are based upon the business rules are still valid.

Tabulated Formats

One of the most popular approaches using tabulated formats is the Framework for Integrated Tests. [MC05] In 2008 Robert C. Martin introduced the Simple List Invocation Method (SLiM) in FitNesse [Mar08b], which provides similar table structures to express requirements. In both approaches there are three commonly used styles: tables that take inputs and check outputs from the system, tables that query the system and check collections of values against the ones obtained from the system under test, and tables that support workflows.

Decision Tables   The first set of tables take input values to the system, execute something in the system, and then check some values from the system against the ones provided. We had such an example in the traffic lights example in SLiM where these are called DecisionTables. In FIT they are called ColumnFixture, and in FitLibrary, an extension for FIT, these tables are called CalculateFixture.

You can express the majority of requirements using a decision table format. The tables for the airport parking lot example are decision tables. The parking duration is the input to the tested system, the parking costs are the output values from the system which the test runner will check. Listing 9.2 shows the airport examples for valet parking formatted as a decision table. Do they look familiar to you?

Listing 9.2 The valet parking tests expressed as a decision table in SLiM

```
 1 !|Parking costs for|Valet Parking |
 2 |parking duration  |parking costs?|
 3 |30 minutes        |$ 12.00       |
 4 |3 hours           |$ 12.00       |
 5 |5 hours           |$ 12.00       |
 6 |5 hours 1 minute  |$ 18.00       |
 7 |12 hours          |$ 18.00       |
 8 |24 hours          |$ 18.00       |
 9 |1 day 1 minute    |$ 36.00       |
10 |3 days            |$ 54.00       |
11 |1 week            |$ 126.00      |
```

There is no restriction to a single input value, nor is there a restriction to check a single output value. In fact, if you leave out the output values, you get a special table for setting up values in the system. This may be handy if you want to describe three accounts that your tests are later going to operate on. See Listing 9.3 for an example. This special decision table without outputs is often called a setup table, or a SetUpFixture.

Listing 9.3 A setup table preparing three different accounts

```
 1 !|Account Creator                              |
 2 |account name   |account state|role            |
 3 |Susi Service   |active       |service user|
 4 |Tim Technician |active       |technician  |
 5 |Uwe Unemployed |unemployed   |service user|
```

While there is no restriction on how many columns your table will have, in practice the readability will heavily suffer if you come up with a table with more than 10 columns. I have seen tests expressed using 30 or so columns with more than hundreds of lines.[1] The problem with these tests is that they are not easy to understand. A future test maintainer—remember this could be you—is unlikely to understand in a few seconds what a particular row is about. This is a test smell that you may want to avoid.[2]

Query Tables Query tables are necessary for collections from the system. In SLiM these are called Query Tables, in FIT they are called RowFixture, and in FitLibrary there are ArrayFixture, SetFixture, and SubsetFixture. Often there is a need to check the order of a collection of entries, or to ensure subsets of entries in a collection. In SLiM they may be prefixed with the word Subset or Ordered to yield the special variants. In FitLibrary there are different classes that you need to subclass from. Listing 9.4 shows an example checking all the users in a system.

Listing 9.4 A query table checking the existence of some previously set up data

```
1 !|Query:Users in the System                          |
2 |user name           |role              |user state|
3 |Tim Tester          |Tester            |active    |
4 |Paul Programmer      |Programmer        |active    |
5 |Petra Projectmanager|Project Manager|active        |
```

Query tables are used after gathering data from the system and receiving a list of different things stored in the system. They come in handy for a collection of accounts in the system, for example, after a search operation. For an online shopping site you can query the shopping cart of your customer and check the contents of the cart against an expected list.

You can check the entries in the collection against just one of their attributes, like the name of an item, or against a combination of name, price, and amount for a shopping cart. Usually the amount of attributes denoted in the table expresses which attributes will be checked. The granularity of your tables then dictates how thoroughly you want to check data from the system.

The more data you express in your tables, the more possible adaptations you have if the name of an attribute changes. For the design of your tests, there is a

---

1. To save some trees I did not include an example—besides that, I refuse to mislead you by showing such a terrible example.
2. From *Refactoring: Improving the Design of Existing Code* [FBB+99] where Fowler and Beck speak of "Design smells" when something is not quite right in the underlying design. The term test smell appears also in *xUnit Test Patterns: Refactoring Test Code* [Mes07].

trade-off between how thoroughly you want to test the application and how much effort you will put into future maintenance of your test suite. On one hand, you may include fewer details in the query tables, leading to a higher risk that something breaks unnoticed by this test. You can tackle this risk by extending the test suite with more examples for the details you left out there or by setting time aside for exploratory testing to attack the risk. Of course, each of these decisions has side effects as well. Another decision could be to include all details you can think of. This may lead to fragile tests if the attributes are renamed, for example. Between these two extremes there are approaches to solve this problem as well. But this also means that you will have to decide the number of details to include in your table structure in your particular situation.

Probably the easiest thing is to go with your first gut feeling and reflect on your decision from time to time. If you find yourself maintaining a lot of tests in your test suite, you should revisit some of your decisions and refactor your test.

Script Tables   You can use script tables to express workflows in your system. You can also use script tables to combine decision tables with query tables in one test. An alternative to the Given-When-Then style of BDD in a tabulated format is a pattern called Setup-Execute-Verify or Arrange-Act-Assert. For Setups I often use DecisionTables without checked outputs in order to set up any precondition in the system. Then I invoke a single operation in a script table, like reloading a balance of the account I just prepared. As a final verification step, I can use a query table to gather all the balances stored at my account and check the values after the reload. You can see a full example in Listing 9.5.

Listing 9.5 A script table with a whole flow through the system

```
 1  !|script|Account Reload|
 2
 3  !|AccountCreator              |
 4  |account name     |tariff |
 5  |prepaid account|prepaid|
 6
 7  |reload|50.00 EUR|on|prepaid account|
 8
 9  !|Query:BalanceChecker|prepaid account|
10  |balance name          |balance value  |
11  |Main balance          |50.00 EUR      |
12  |Bonus balance         |5.00 EUR       |
```

Script Tables from SLiM are named ActionFixture in FIT, or DoFixture in FitLibrary. In general, you can express anything you want in your test table with them. The tools use a convention for calling particular functions in your glue code based upon how you wrote your examples. This is highly dependent on the particular tool you chose. Usually there is a way to separate parameters to the function from the text. The text is concatenated–camel-cased[3]–to derive the name of the function to call.

Script tables are useful whenever you want to express larger sets of operations. For example, you can express to start a system, input some values, click a button, and then check some values before finally shutting down the system again using script tables. You may often want to use a combination of different tables in your tests.

Keyword-Driven Automation

You can use keywords to express combinations of operations in a single one. The operation that combines several keywords becomes a higher level operation at that time. You can virtually combine multiple levels of keywords to match the right level of abstraction for your tests.

In the traffic lights example we used the `invalid combination` scenario to express a higher level concept in its own keyword (see Listing 9.6). In the test execution report we could also dive into the trace of this keyword. Another popular framework built on keywords is RobotFramework.[4] RobotFramework comes with a rich number of test libraries and provides add-ons for web-based tests, SSH support, databases, and Swing.

Listing 9.6 The usage of a scenario table as a keyword in the traffic lights example (repeat of Listing 7.15)

```
1 ...
2 !2 Invalid combinations
3
4 !|scenario        |invalid combination|firstLight||secondLight|
5 |set first light |@firstLight                                 |
6 |set second light|@secondLight                                |
7 |execute                                                      |
```

---

3. Camel-casing refers to a method to concatenate fluent text to a function name that does not include whitespace. For example, the text `This is fun` would yield `thisIsFun` as a function name.
4. http://robotframework.org

```
 8 |check          |first light   |yellow blink              |
 9 |check          |second light  |yellow blink              |
10
11 !|script|FirstLightSwitchingCrossingController|
12
13 !|invalid combination    |
14 |firstLight   |secondLight|
15 |green        |red, yellow|
16 |green        |green      |
17 |green        |yellow     |
18 |yellow       |red, yellow|
19 |yellow       |green      |
20 |yellow       |yellow     |
21 |red, yellow  |red, yellow|
22 |red, yellow  |green      |
23 |red, yellow  |yellow     |
24 |red          |red, yellow|
25 |red          |green      |
26 |red          |yellow     |
27 |yellow blink |red        |
28 |yellow blink |red, yellow|
29 |yellow blink |green      |
30 |yellow blink |yellow     |
```

When using keywords, the border between test data representation and test automation code becomes fluent. You may have keywords implemented in a programming language driving the application or interacting on a lower level with the operating system. You may as well have keywords that are constructed by a combination of lower-level keywords. And you may also combine these higher-level keywords in new ways. With this organization you get multiple levels of keywords.

This approach is a powerful way to organize your test data around a set of low-level test automation drivers. With new combinations of keywords the language for your test automation code evolves and becomes even more powerful. On the downside, this approach may lead to deep and complex levels of test automation keywords. At the time of this writing there were few refactoring tools for keywords available. Maintaining several levels of keywords then can become a mess. Although it should be simple to search and replace text in some files, the fluent style of this test data makes it complicated to find every occurrence. Renaming a keyword, for example, or extending the parameter list of a keyword becomes difficult. Most modern IDEs for programming languages support these refactorings now in a safe way. In the long run we will hopefully see more refactoring tools for keyword-driven automation as well—eventually even refactoring across lower-level and higher-level keywords at the same time.

Glue Code and Support Code

How your examples get automated heavily depends on the framework in use. For example, for Java some frameworks rely on Java annotations to find the code to execute for a given phrase in the example. Other frameworks use camel-cased function names. Some frameworks support the usage of bean methods—getters and setters for properties in your classes, like first name and last name of an account.

Regardless of the framework or tool you use for automating your examples, you should take into account that you are developing your glue code. Some teams seem oblivious to the fact that they are developing code while writing the glue and support code. When you wire up your application to the tests, the code you write may seem simple and easy to maintain. Over time your growing code base will become hard to maintain if you don't apply similar principles to the design of your glue and support code as you would apply to your production code.

For me this usually means starting with a simple code base. I want to be able to start automated acceptance tests fast. For one client we were able to come up with some automated tests on the acceptance level after spending roughly two hours with two persons on it. Two more hours, and we had a basic understanding of the driver code for our automated tests, as well as a basic glue code layer through which we could run most of our acceptance tests. We were aware that this code would be extended once we got more complex automated tests later.

Over time, when more and more functionality starts to grow, I consider actively extracting new components from the existing code. As we saw in Part II with the `LightStateEditor`, we added these components using test-driven development. We actually tested our test code. When I worked at one company, we actually applied several code metrics like static code analysis and code coverage for our automation code. We had a separate project with a separate build in our Continuous Integration system. When we compared the metrics to the ones from our production code, we were outperforming the production code with our test code. That test automation code was still in use and development two years later.

If this sounds rather extreme to you, consider the following story I heard in 2009. The team had a visit from an external contractor on software test automation. The contractor felt uncomfortable adding more support code with complex logic. So, he used test-driven development for the complex code that he was adding.

After the contractor left again, the code coverage of the whole application had risen by 10% to a total of 15%.

Developing test automation code is software development. Therefore, you should apply the same principles to your glue and support code that you apply to developing your production code. In the past I have seen test automation code that lacked design, was not well documented, and was sometimes even fragile with bugs in it. When we developed a new test automation approach at one company, we overcame all these drawbacks in the test automation code by applying incremental design together with test-driven development. Test-driven development helped us to understand the code while it also provided the necessary documentation. By using TDD we also ensured that our test automation code did not suffer from bugs, thereby leading to false positives—tests that pass although the software is broken—or false negatives—tests that fail though the software is working—when running our automated tests.

The necessity for adding unit tests to your glue and support code becomes obvious if you use ATDD in the way we used it in Part II. While working with the acceptance tests, we discovered the domain of the application. With the knowledge and experience with the domain we could easily extract or derive the domain code from the glue code. Without unit tests for the glue code at that time, we would add unit tests either by extraction first, then adding tests after the fact, or by developing new domain code using test-driven development.

The Right Format

There is something to say for the right format. The formats that I have shown, behavior-driven development, tabulated formats, and keyword-based examples, represent the variety of formats that were around when I wrote this book. In the past decade most of the tools available today underwent a development to support tests in either format shown here. For example, you can use a tabulated format using FitNesse's SLiM framework with decision and query tables. Alternately, you can use a Given-When-Then format with SLiM by using script tables. For Robot Framework there are similar ways to use one of the three presented formats. For your particular combination of test data format—BDD, tables, or keywords—and test automation language there is probably at least one framework around that you can get started with.

This is great, since you can focus your attention on using the right format to express examples for your application in the most natural style and delay the tool decision until later. Most teams that started with an implementation of a particular tool just got that: an implementation of a tool, but not an implementation of a successful approach [Adz11]. Obviously, an automated testing tool is not a vital test strategy [KBP01].

For your examples as well as for your tests, once you have automated the examples there are several stakeholders. First, there is the programmer of the feature who needs to understand the example from the written description. Then there is the programmer who will automate the particular example. Your customer or product owner is also going to read through the test once it's automated during the review. Your whole team might also consult your tests when the next extension is planned in several iterations in order to understand side effects. Finally, there is the future maintainer of the system who will adapt the test cases when necessary.

All these stakeholders should be able to quickly understand the intent of your example and your tests. In order to do this, they need to be able to read the tests and understand their context and specific focus. The longer it takes to read and understand a test, the more time is wasted in the sense of lean thinking. From a systemic point of view, more wasted time leads to less time for productive work. The less productive work, the more perceived pressure you will feel from the outside. The more pressure you feel, the more likely you take shortcuts to your tests. The more shortcuts you take, the less understandable your tests become (see Figure 9.1). At this point, you formed a vicious cycle, or downward spiral. You seem doomed.

You can break this vicious cycle by realizing the role you play in this system. There is one obvious decision point in this cycle that influences whether the

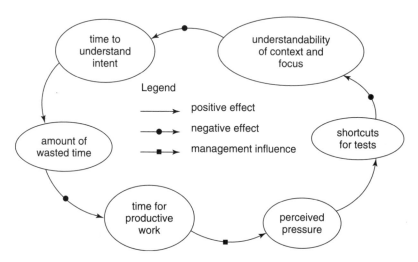

Figure 9.1 A systems view on intent-revealing tests

described system is a vicious cycle or a positive feedback loop leading to a balanced system: the decision to waste time on reading acceptance tests [Wei91].

If you reverse this decision, you spend less time trying to understand your tests. The less time you spend, the more time you gain for productive work. This relieves you from outside pressure and prevents you from taking shortcuts in your tests.

Teams use acceptance tests as a communication device. The variety of stakeholders makes this transparent. While the application is under development, there is a permanent handover from one team member to another. Successful teams ensure readability of their tests to reduce the friction that such handovers cause. In 2009 I heard a story from Enrique Comba-Riepenhausen, who said that his on-site customer could read not only his acceptance tests, but also his unit tests and even his domain code. His team had successfully implemented a concept that Eric Evans calls ubiquitous language [Eva03].

Every project shares a common language, a ubiquitous language. The more translation between different languages that is necessary in a project, the more potential for confusion exists. If the business domain is expressed using the same terms in your acceptance tests, you ensure that your customer will also understand your tests. If you also model your domain code around the same language, you ensure that everyone reaches the same understanding while avoiding confusions later once it's too late.

Refine the Examples

Getting essential examples from your customer or product owner helps you getting started with the functionality. Unfortunately, a first discussion as we saw it in Part I might not give you all the examples that you need in order to build the software. You need to refine your examples after having identified a first set of it [Adz11].

Refinement of examples may happen in several ways. Usually, testers know how to flesh out hidden assumptions and boundary conditions from their first examples. Depending on the domain of the application, there may be constraints for a maximum length of a string, different validation rules, or combinations of business rules that exclude each other. If you miss these conditions in the initial Specification Workshop meeting, it pays to ask a tester to refine the examples.

Another case of refinement of examples is a particular business rule that the product owner was not sure about. After getting a clarification about the underlying business rules the product owner, a tester, and a programmer get together to refine the examples they identified in the first sitting. With the additional information, they can now extend the rough examples to form a more complete picture of the functionality.

As a tester, you will naturally apply boundary conditions, domain partitioning, or equivalence classes to refine examples. In fact, any testing technique may help to refine the examples and seek for gaps. The following section presents a brief discussion of testing techniques you may want to keep in mind while refining your examples. A full discussion of the techniques is well beyond the scope of this book. If you are looking for more details on testing techniques, you may want to take a closer look at Lee Copeland's *A Practitioner's Guide to Software Test Design* [Cop04] or Kaner's *Testing Computer Software* [KFN99].

Domain Testing

In domain testing, tests are broken down from a larger domain into smaller sub-domains. Values that are fed into the system are partitioned into several classes where the system behaves the same way. These classes are called equivalence classes. We saw this in the airport example. The first equivalence class was the split among the different parking lots. The next classes were derived from the business rules. Usually, there was one class for the first few hours, one class for the first few days, and finally one class for weeks. Within each of these classes we picked one example exactly at the boundary, at least one right in the middle, and one value right before the next boundary and put them into the set of examples.

Let's consider the example of the long-term surface parking lot. The business rules describe costs of $2.00 per hour, $10.00 daily maximum, and $60.00 per week. The first equivalence class within this parking lot is the behavior for the first day up to the fifth hour. We pick examples for one hour, three hours, and five hours. Up from the fifth hour we have the second equivalence class up to the end of that day. We may pick five hours and one minute, ten hours, and twenty-four hours from this class. Now, we may pick to repeat similar values for the second day, too, so that we can observe that this condition holds there as well. This then becomes a combination of the first two equivalence classes. However, the behavior should be the same for the second as for the third or fourth day in this class. Finally, when we hit the weekly maximum at the end of the sixth day, we should get another equivalence class for the whole seventh day, which in turn may be combined with multiple weeks as well.

Taking a look back at the results after the workshop, the values reflect this partitioning (see Table 9.1). The first five values fall into the first equivalence class for hourly rates. The next four illustrations represent examples from the second equivalence class, sometimes combined with the first equivalence class of hourly payment. The final six illustrations represent examples form the third equivalence class, sometimes combined with the former two equivalence classes.

Table 9.1 Long-Term Surface Parking
Examples at the End of the Workshop

Parking Duration	Parking Costs
30 minutes	$2.00
1 hour	$2.00
5 hours	$10.00
6 hours	$10.00
24 hours	$10.00
1 day, 1 hour	$12.00
1 day, 3 hours	$16.00
1 day, 6 hours	$20.00
6 days	$60.00
6 days, 1 hour	$60.00
7 days	$60.00
1 week, 2 days	$80.00
3 weeks	$180.00

Boundary Values

Testing for boundary values becomes easy when combined with a domain analysis
beforehand. The idea is that at each of the boundaries for the equivalence classes
errors are likely to occur. Traditional theory therefore suggests to test one value
right in front of the boundary, one at the boundary, and one beyond the boundary.
To me this seems to be basic math, and looking at the example from before we
seem to have applied it in a reasonable manner with some freedom.

Consider the airport example. In the case of the valet parking costs, there were
two equivalence classes—one in which you would be charged $18.00, and another
one in which you get charged $12.00. The boundary value here is five hours. Using
this information, we should consider one test for exactly five hours (the boundary
value), one case for less then five hours, i.e., four hours and 59 minutes, and one
just above this boundary value, i.e., five hours and one minute (see Table 9.2).

Table 9.2 Boundary Values for Valet Parking

Parking Duration	Parking Costs
4 hours 59 minutes	$12.00
5 hours	$12.00
5 hours 1 minute	$18.00

Of course, there are more (hidden) boundary values like a parking duration of zero minutes. The value of testers in specification workshops comes from seeing such hidden boundaries and equivalence classes that otherwise will be assumed between the business and the development.

Pairwise Testing

Pairwise Testing is based on the observation that errors often happen for a combination of two different input values. If our application has an input A with values a1, a2, and a3 and an input B with values b1, b2, and b3, we can achieve great confidence with the test cases in Table 9.3.

If we add a third variable to our system C with the values c1 and c2, we end up with the test cases listed in Table 9.4.

Table 9.3 Pairwise Testing Examples

A	B
a1	b1
a1	b2
a1	b3
a2	b1
a2	b2
a2	b3
a3	b1
a3	b3
a3	b3

Table 9.4 Pairwise Testing Examples with Three Variables

A	B	C
a1	b1	c1
a1	b2	c2
a1	b3	c2
a2	b1	c1
a2	b2	c1
a2	b3	c2
a3	b1	c2
a3	b3	c1
a3	b3	c1

Table 9.5 Pairwise Testing Examples for the Parking Lot Example

Weeks	Days	Hours
0	0	0
1	0	1
3	0	3
1	1	0
0	1	1
0	1	3
3	1	5
3	3	0
0	3	1
1	3	3
3	6	1
0	6	5
1	6	6
1	7	5
0	7	6
3	7	0
3	0	6
1	0	5
3	1	6
0	3	5
1	3	6
3	6	0
0	6	3
3	7	1
1	7	3

The algorithm ensured that all combinations of each pair of variables are chosen as a test case. For combinatorial problems, this approach helps to reduce the amount of tests that you have to run while ensuring a basic coverage.

For the airport parking lot example, we can apply this approach to the equivalence classes. For example, I might take examples for 0, 1, and 3 weeks, for 0, 1, 3, 6, and 7 days, and for 0, 1, 3, 5, and 6 hours. The pairwise algorithm will then come up with the test cases as listed in Table 9.5.

You might note that we still have to calculate the output values for the parking costs in this example. I will leave this as an exercise for the reader.

Cut Examples

Over time your test suite will grow larger and larger. There seem to be two magic boundaries, depending on how fast your test suites execute.

The first boundary exists when you reach an overall duration of more than several minutes. Before this happens, you feel comfortable getting feedback from your test suite regularly. You execute your tests nearly as often as your unit tests. But when the acceptance test suite starts to take more than about ten(-ish) minutes, you start to get annoyed by the long execution times. You run your tests less regularly, most often once for every check-in, but seldom more. By doing so, you actively delay the feedback you can get from your tests. This comes with the risk of introducing bugs into your code base that go unnoticed for some time. When working in a development team, this may even lead to confusion if someone integrates the faulty code into his or her latest changes.

The second magic boundary exists at an execution time of about two to three hours for your regression test suite. Lisa Crispin commented that her team strives to keep their automated non-unit tests below a 45-minute boundary—otherwise programmers will stop paying attention to the results. Up to this point you can safely execute your tests. Behind this boundary, tests seem to start to degenerate. More and more tests fail in the continuous integration system [DMG07]. At this point, you slowly start to rerun more and more failed tests from the nightly build as part of your daily work. This eats up more and more of your time, giving you less and less time for new tests or to fix problems in the existing ones. Just like slowly boiled frogs, you become more and more obsessed by the Backward Blindfold [Wei01, page 125]

> The fish is always the last to see the water.

In order to prevent this, you should seek opportunities to speed up your tests. This might mean reorganizing your acceptance tests so that they execute against a lower-level interface—for example, using the model in a MVC architecture instead of the user interface or view. You may also seek opportunities to mock out some portions of the slower subsystems like a database or a third-party component. This works just fine for some time but comes with at least two serious trade-offs. First of all, you create a larger gap between the application that your tests exercise and the application that users are facing. In the next section "Consider Gaps," we will cover this risk. The second risk is that you will have fewer options to cut your examples at the next time you hit a boundary for your test execution time. When you have run out of options to speed up your executable examples, the only option you may have left is the Queen of Hearts' option in Lewis Carroll's *Alice's Adventures in Wonderland*: Off with their heads [Car65].

While this may sound extreme, regression testing eventually just finds 23% of the problems [Jon07]. Automated regression tests find a minority of the bugs [KBP01]. Since your examples might serve as regression tests, you are probably fine keeping the 23% that actually catch all the regressions that you're interested in. Of course, the problem is that you will seldom know which of the tests give you the 23% of regression failures before implementing them. That's why teams start building up a large set of tests. While this might give you a warm and cozy feeling about confidence for some time, when you hit the second boundary of execution time with your regression test suite, it is surely getting in your way.

I remember a project where we had a regression test suite that executed for about 36 hours. We didn't know exactly how long it took to execute it, since we were not able to execute the whole test suite in a single run. While the number of regression tests seemed overwhelming, the sheer number of tests was no longer serving any purpose at all. Two months later we had cut off the regression test to the 10% that provided us with quick feedback if something was broken, and thereby shortened the feedback loop for our regression test suite. Needless to say, that we would have been doomed without such a step.

When cutting down examples initially, standard testing techniques might serve you well. In retrospect, with the 36-hour test suite, we might have used a pairwise approach to cut down the examples. To recall the subsection in Chapter 9 "Pairwise Testing," the pairwise approach relies on combining any two factors together once. The number of tests to execute may be reduced drastically while still providing a warm and cozy coverage of the underlying business rules.

If you already applied some cut-down techniques like combinatorial reduction, and still face a five-hour test execution time, you may want to separate even more tests. Some teams start to organize their automated tests into smaller suites by using tags for certain risk areas. You may tag some of your tests for smoke testing and apply a staged build [DMG07] to your test suites. With a staged build you execute a small set of tests that address the most high-risk areas first. If all of them succeed, you execute the larger set of tests next to address areas that were overlooked.

Finally, some teams even automate all the examples in the iteration in parallel to the production code. Once the tests pass, they delete most of the tests, eventually leaving a very basic set of regression tests for the automated test suite. Gojko Adzic had several such examples when he interviewed 50 teams in 2010 on their usage of Specification by Example [Adz11]. Effectively, the teams pushed their test execution times in front of the first boundary. They enabled themselves for rapid feedback while sacrificing the coverage they got from their automated tests—or stopped pretending such a coverage in first place. This approach is fine as long as you consider all the gaps.

Consider Gaps

When automating testing, we should consider which bugs we are not finding while automating [KBP01]. This lesson from software testing is mostly concerned about opportunity costs of test automation. For any test that we automate, there is a set of tests that we will not run—no matter whether they are automated or manual tests.

Speaking of gaps in your ATDD approach, you have to find the right balance for automating tests versus running manual tests for areas and risks that your automated tests will not cover. Test automation alone leads to an unbalanced approach. Consider, for example, an application where you can enter personal information for your clients. Your automated tests cover the creation of one client, the business rules for creating the client, and field interdependencies like invalid zip codes or a mismatch between zip code and city.

In this hypothetical scenario you don't run any manual tests, and when your application gets released to your customers, and they start using it, you get lots of complaints. Almost all of them state that your application is hard to use since the order for navigating through your application is unnatural. If you enter a single data value, the problem does not become apparent, but if you have to enter thousands of client records, you will get screwed.

Once I had to use such an application. The problem was the tab-order for the fields in the data entry page. When I entered the last name, hit tab, the cursor would change to the birthday before switching to the first name. Previously, we had a DOS-based application in use, where the tab-ordering was not a problem at all. When switching to an application under Windows, and migrating the 300 accounts, I noticed the problem and got fed up with it pretty quickly.

What should you do if you were the vendor of that application? Of course, you could describe the tab-ordering feature using examples and automate these examples. With every change to the code base you could capture these sort of bugs. The problem is that such a test would be heavily bound to the particular implementation of the user interface. With every new field in your input screen you would probably have to change that test.

The alternative would be to schedule a time-boxed session of exploratory testing [KFN99]. In such a session you could explore the usability of your interface design. With every change to the user interface you would schedule a similar session to explore the usability of the new screen layout again.

Facing these two alternatives, almost all attendees of my courses and workshops explained that they would go for the exploratory alternative. Reasons for this include the creation and maintenance costs for the automated tests and the return on that investment.

While this may seem like an exceptional example, Jurgen Appelo teaches in his course on Management and Leadership the Unknown-Unknowns Fallacy. Pretending to have covered all risks is a trap that many managers fall into [App11]. Scientists believed for centuries that all swans were white. The first occurrence of a black swan proved them wrong. Hard to predict and rare events can have high impact [Tal10]. In fact thinking that disaster is impossible more often than not leads to an unthought disaster. Jerry Weinberg coined the term Titanic Effect [Wei91].

If you think that you considered all the gaps, you probably forget the black swan, the unknown-unknown. Despite relying on a single approach to test your software, compensate for the possibility that test automation alone will not solve all your problems. There will be gaps in your testing concert, and you as the conductor should bring the right orchestra to the audience.

Build Your Testing Orchestra

The testing quadrants as discussed in detail in Lisa Crispin and Janet Gregory's *Agile Testing* [CG09] book and first described by Brian Marick [Mar03] might reveal additional testing activities to yield a balanced approach to your application. In brief, testing activities can be split along two dimensions. The first dimension covers tests that either support your team on your project or critique the product's value to the customer. The second dimension spreads orthogonally between technical tests versus business-facing tests (see Figure 9.2).

The testing quadrants separate activities along four quadrants. The first quadrant covers technical tests that support the team. Unit tests and intermodule integration tests on a low level usually fall into this category. In the second quadrant are tests that support the team and have a business focus. These tests include automated acceptance tests as covered in this book. The third quadrant concerns business-facing tests that critique the product. Some examples for these are alpha and beta tests, but also user acceptance tests, usability tests, and Exploratory Testing. The fourth quadrant reminds us about those tests that critique the product, but face a more technical level. The most prominent test techniques in this quadrant include performance, load, and stress tests.

As you can see, acceptance tests that you create as a side effect to ATDD are concerned with the second quadrant. If you focus on the business-level tests that support your team alone, you are likely to miss performance problems, usability, or simple problems in your code quality that will cause you pain in the long run.[5]

---

5. In the literature this is often called Technical Debt. The term was coined in 1992 by Ward Cunningham: http://c2.com/cgi/wiki?TechnicalDebt

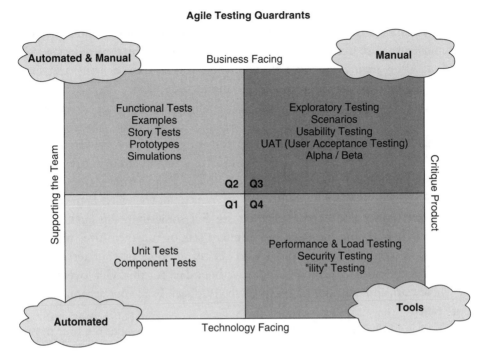

Figure 9.2 The testing quadrants can help you realize gaps in your testing approach

Not covering these three areas leaves your application and your project vulnerable to a lot of risks.

Finally, if you don't agree with me on this, you may check out the parking lot calculator page. It is a real page based on real requirements. The requirements are fulfilled in the version I reference in this book. Although all the acceptance tests pass, there are subtle and even obvious bugs in the calculator. See how many you can find within half an hour, then come back and read this section again, and see if the experience changed your mind about it.

Summary

When thinking about getting started with ATDD, play around with different ways to express your data. Try writing down your examples in a tabulated form, then change it to BDD-style. When you come up with a representation that makes sense to you, your team, and your business representative, only then start to look for a framework that could suite your purpose. Also, you should make it a team decision on which framework to pick. You should also keep in mind that different drivers

for your application—for example Selenium or Watir for web pages, SWTBot for
SWT applications—have different side-effects. Start with the most promising guess,
implement one test from end to end, and then think about reconsidering your
decision. After getting some initial experience, you will see benefits and some
drawbacks, and can come up with a better informed decision.

Getting down the first set of examples usually is not enough. Use test design
knowledge to refine your initial set of examples. Boundary values, pair-wise
approaches, and domain testing can help you with that and your testers should
know about such techniques. If you want to learn more about test design techniques,
take a look into "A Practitioner's Guide to Software Test Design". [Cop04]

Over time your test suite should grow. At some point you will face the problem
that it takes too long to execute all the tests. For some time you might be able
to stick with separating the tests into different sets or run them over night. But
eventually you will find that you have to get rid of some of your tests. Ninety
minutes execution time seems to be a magic boundary for this. Get together with
the whole team and talk about ways to get the feedback from your acceptance tests
more timely.

There might be gaps in your overall testing strategy. Consider the four testing
quadrants and if you covered every necessary point in the quadrants: Do you run
exploratory tests regularly? When did you invite a user for some usability testing
the last time? What about load and performance testing? ATDD addresses just
the business-facing quadrant that shall help your team move forward. Acceptance
tests are an essential part that most teams leave out, but you shouldn't sacrifice too
much from the other quadrants as well.

Chapter 10
Specify Collaboratively

Traditional software specifications come with one problem: They need special care to do them well. Once you have nailed them down, though, they quickly become obsolete for different reasons that you may be able to influence or not. For example, if a competitor releases a new feature in its software, your requirements may change in an instant in order to keep your market share. Since this is clearly a nontechnical decision, someone with a business background has to at least participate in that decision.

The more diverse opinions you can get in your requirements process, the clearer the picture of the application gets. In general, there are at least three different perspectives that you should include. On the one hand, there is the business perspective. On agile teams, this perspective is usually represented by a customer representative, a customer proxy, or in Scrum it's the ProductOwner.

On the other hand, there is the technical perspective. On more traditional teams, a lead programmer or technical leader might represent this viewpoint. On agile teams you may want to include at least one team member who knows the code base from working with the source code.

Finally, you need someone to mediate between the two perspectives. In traditional projects you will find business analysts bringing in this viewpoint. An experienced software tester can bring the same value as well.

Meet the Power of Three

But why do these three different perspectives help in specifying the application? Designing a software system comes with many decisions between two aspects: the business functions and the technical constraints. Our software code bases are full of trade-off decisions between these functions and constraints. Our bug databases, on the other hand, are full of reports where the decisions were plain wrong.

Some of these decisions are hard to change during the software development process, and some of them are easy to fix. By getting the two different viewpoints of business functions and technical constraints together early, we help to find the right trade-off decisions early so that as few as possible of the always hard-to-fix bugs as well as the always easy-to-fix bugs are introduced. Incidentally, we can also avoid all the bugs in between these two extremes.

The functions for a software system span a solution space [GW89]. In this solution space there are many possible designs that fulfill the required functions. They also explain how you can explore the solution space with different attributes for the functions like performance or load behavior. These attributes constrain the amount of possible solutions to the space of solutions that is desired by the customer.

On the other hand, there are constraints to the technology that is used to realize the software. These constraints restrict the amount of possible designs that fulfill the functions and attributes.

Bringing the business functions and attributes together with the technical constraints early helps the participants with exploring the space for possible designs. This is one of the key ingredients for the approach of acceptance test-driven development that make it work. And it turns out that testers can facilitate this exploration process with their ability to question and challenge functions, attributes, and constraints of the software.

But what about the independent viewpoint that a separate test team can bring to the table? Through decades of testing training we have learned and taught that programmers and testers should work completely independently from the same basis, the requirements document. This avoids the phenomenon that modern psychology coined confirmation bias. A tester should be unbiased by the viewpoints of the programmer and critique the product when appropriate. Some teams interpret this rule to the degree that programmers and testers are not allowed to talk to each other at all.

Specifying the software together with a programmer does not make the tester preoccupied. Instead programmers and testers work together with the business experts to trawl the requirements for the software. If you think this biases the opinion of a tester, then you should start to wonder whether reading the same requirements document biases your testers as well. Specifying examples together with programmers and business experts is the same as attending a requirements workshop—something that most testers dream of for all their professional career.

In fact, the teams that Gojko Adzic interviewed for his book *Specification by Example* [Adz11] reported that the added viewpoints of at least one programmer and one tester lead to a better understanding of the requirements right from the start. As we saw in the airport example, the conversation led to situations in which the programmers contributed through technical questions of the business process, and also questions from the tester supported the understandability and visualization of the requirements with the table structure.

During the iterations both programmers and testers work from the same basic understanding of the feature. The examples identified as acceptance tests serve the team as verification of their progress.

For the best results these three different roles should be included: a business expert like the ProductOwner or an on-site customer, a programmer, and a tester. Based on the number of roles involved, Janet Gregory and Lisa Crispin call this the Power of Three.

The *Rule of Three Interpretations* [Wei93, page 90] reminds us to think of at least three different possibilities before concluding upon something that we received.

> If I can't think of at least three different interpretations of what I received, I haven't thought enough about what it might mean.

The Power of Three helps in overcoming this shortcoming of imagination. By bringing three different perspectives to the table, your potential to have thought enough about the requirements of the feature or story rises dramatically. That's what makes the Power of Three so powerful.

The Power of Three goes beyond functional requirements as well. The programmer knows the performance liabilities of the code base and might ask for clarification on this. The testers are usually aware of usability shortcomings. Programmer, tester, and business representative can get clarification on the quality attributes of the upcoming features—these are sometimes referred to as the nonfunctional requirements. Remember to consider the gaps you leave with your automated tests and build a complete testing orchestra (see Chapter 9, "Build Your Testing Orchestra") using the testing quadrants (see Figure 9.2). Most of the performance, load, and stability requirements can be checked using test automation as well.

Hold Workshops

As we saw in Part I, a workshop can help the whole team to reach a shared understanding of the functionality that it is going to implement. There are some things you will have to keep in mind in order to make these workshops a success for everyone, regardless of whether they are participating.

Participants

First of all, you should make sure that you pick the right participants. For some teams this may mean involving the whole development team as well as customers from different companies. These teams usually have a larger meeting, but will meet for a workshop every other iteration.

On the other hand, there are teams that just include three roles in the workshop, leading to a small meeting of three persons. In any case, you should include diverse viewpoints. Usually this means including someone who is familiar with the business side of the product. You also want to have easy access to an expert user [Coc06].

As I showed in "Meet the Power of Three," you should include at least one programmer and one tester as well. A programmer knows the code base. Based on the discussion that arises at a specification workshop, the programmer will ask questions regarding the technical implementation of the functionality at hand. By their very nature, programmers will be concerned about how the function can be implemented and have the domain model already in place in their head. The workshop brings them the benefit of reaching a common understanding of the business domain for the new functionality.

Testers with their critical mindset can find gaps in the business rules quickly. Another unique ability testers put into a specification workshop is their ability to make business rules transparent through tables. Whether they have been using a so-called Agile-friendly automation framework before, an experienced tester knows about decision tables and how to describe complex business rules using a tabular representation. If you develop such a representation in the specification workshop together, programmers, testers, and business experts reach agreement on the discussed functionality even before any source code is touched.

Goal of the Workshop

For specification workshops to become a success, it's relevant to know your primary audience. The development team—that is, programmers and testers—are the primary audience, while the domain expert brings in the necessary knowledge about the upcoming features. It's essential to keep in mind that customers and external business experts are probably short on time [Adz09]. If you invite them to a meeting where your programmers fight for whether to use the latest web server technology, and which one that should be, you are probably not going to get their participation for the next workshop.

Rather than discuss technical issues in your implementation, you will need an experienced facilitator who focuses the attention on the features. The goal of the workshop is to reach a common understanding of the business rules. You can still discuss all the technical issues later when the business representatives are not attending. The time spent in the specification workshop should be used to reach a common picture.

Frequency and Duration

This leads to the question of how often you should conduct such a workshop. Of course, this depends heavily on the availability of your domain experts. If you need access to some business representatives, you may find out that these are rather busy. On the other hand, you may have an onsite customer whom you can ask additional questions on a daily basis.

Depending on your particular context, you can set aside time for a specification workshop once in a month, or once shortly before the next iteration starts.

Based on how frequently you run specification workshops with your domain expert, you will set aside different time frames. If you run your specification workshop less frequently, you may either want to discuss more features, and therefore set aside more time for the discussion. On the other hand, if you want to leave the meetings short and still meet less frequently, you may either choose to discuss fewer features, or to do some up-front preparation.

In case you want to discuss fewer features, you should work through your backlog of planned features according to the most current priorization. The features that you will most likely include in the next iteration should be discussed first. You may also want to leave out features that are clear for the team, such as a login function or a comment text field for a web page. This leaves you more time to discuss challenging business rules in more complex features.

In case you want to do some up-front preparation, you can work through your backlog of ideas before the workshop and come up with questions for the business expert to answer. You can create a list of open questions during a backlog grooming meeting, which most Scrum teams hold. You may also set aside a separate meeting to discuss upcoming features in brevity a few days before the workshop. Another way to generate some ideas and open questions for the business rules are meetings that create a visualization from the understanding up front, and collect open questions in a mindmap. Although you should keep in mind that once you turn on the video projector in the specification workshop and start to collect the answers in the mindmap as well, your meeting will suffer dramatically while you force everyone to sit silently watching at all of your typos on the video projection. Usually, technology on a lower level, such as index cards, whiteboard, or flipcharts, prevent you from such inefficient meetings if you pick one facilitator to record the answers for you.

Trawl Requirements

Requirements are usually not gathered [Coh04]. Customers and business experts think they know precisely what they want. But when they see the end results, your team finds out that they wanted something completely different.

This is where the metaphor of gathering requirements does not hold. You could gather requirements if they would be lying obviously for everyone to pick and take away in order to produce the desired piece of software. Unfortunately, requirements do not lie around waiting to be picked up. Most teams have to learn this the hard way.

Mike Cohn suggests to use a different metaphor instead. Since requirements are not lying around waiting to be gathered together, we need to do something to get a hold of them. There are techniques that help you do that on different levels, just like a fishnet can have different netting sizes in order to catch different sorts of fish while letting others swim through. This analogy holds wonderfully for the different techniques of specification by example.

In the examples earlier we saw two widespread ways for working with specification by example. The first was to have a separate testing group that can work in parallel with the programmers on a given feature for the software. In this scenario our fishnet consists of reaching a common understanding on the features before starting any work to incorporate these features into the existing product.

The team got together and trawled for the requirements of the parking lot. Since everyone had a basic understanding of parking a car, team members could reach a common understanding for parking costs at the airport by asking questions. These questions served to fish for examples. Tony, the tester, quickly found out that he can illustrate the understanding of the business rules with written examples. While writing them down, Phyllis and Bill could see, in terms of their discussion, what their fishnet was still missing.

Later the team reduced the examples to a minimum. During this discussion those examples helped everyone to understand what really is necessary. The reduction of the examples helped those to make the size of the fishnet more coarse and let more fish pass through.

The result is a fishnet for requirements that lets some uninteresting requirements through, like mackerel fish while catching all the barracuda. On the other hand, the net makes sure to catch the carps and pickerels if you are more interested in these.

In the second example we saw that collaborative settings are not the only opportunity to trawl for requirements. In the traffic light example we dug for additional information on the business domain before starting to implement anything. Since we were the only ones working on the codebase, we could apply a different way to trawl for requirements. We used a method I deliberately call just-in-time requirements trawling. While the code base grew and grew more, we could think the requirements through once we ran out of examples.

This is a pattern that not only works when you develop code on a two-person team, but also on multi-person teams. While you may have an initial understanding of the domain, I found thinking through concrete examples to express my understanding a big help in digging deeper. More than that, the thinking process helps you see different implementations and design solutions for the domain model in the code.

As the code base grows, my understanding of the problem domain evolves as well. I learn about the application and its intended use. Indeed, we procrastinated on designing the domain model in our code in order to make a more informed decision about the domain model.

One could argue that we could have seen that design right from the start of the discussion. A well-experienced designer could have foreseen where the code base would be going. This is true to a certain degree. At the point where I had the impression that we were up to something, we stopped in order to reflect on the current code base. This reflection helped us pick the right net for the trawl of requirements. As the design for the crossing controller later showed, we also may find that we caught all the jelly fish instead of the carps. Taking a step back from this experience, and learning from it, is a sure way to let experience teach you anything at all.

Reflection also helps you to pick the right netting for your nets when trawling for requirements. Most successful teams started with a basic simple approach [Adz11]. During the first few months of implementing the first approach, the teams noticed a shortcoming in the process. They reflected on it and adapted it to match their particular situation.

In order to find the right granularity for creating your requirements trawling nets, you will have to start with an approach, gather experience while applying it, and reflect on the experiences you had in order to learn and adapt from it. If your team does retrospectives regularly, then you might have experienced the learning and adaptation process.

Summary

Three different perspectives on the requirements will help you to find the right ones. Customers, programmers, and testers can come up with great decisions for this. If you organize your requirements trawling in workshops, you will gain the viewpoints from all the different roles in your team. Also, make sure to try out your current net and learn from the experience that you will get.

Chapter 11
Automate Literally

After you worked hard on trawling together the examples for your application, it would be a waste of time if you directly threw them away without using them for your advantage—or even worse, you could put them in a document and wait for the dust to cover the print-out. Instead, a wiser approach for you would be to use your examples in order to drive your test automation efforts. If you can automate your examples to the degree that you can use it during an iteration demonstration or general product demonstration, your business representative will recognize the previously agreed upon examples.

Now you can achieve this recognition with a friendly automation approach. Friendly automation enables you to automate the examples as literally as possible. This means that you may reformat your examples in order to fit a certain table layout, but you can keep the textual portions of the examples almost to the letter.

In the airport parking lot example we saw literal automation. Tony reused the examples Bill, Phyllis, and he had agreed upon previously in the workshop. Using friendly automation he could automate these examples nearly to the letter.

One could argue that Tony had written down the examples in a format suitable for automation in first place. Indeed, he could have become biased by the tools that are around for Agile-friendly test automation. On the other hand, the tables also could have been influenced by traditional decision tables, assuming as a tester he knows about them.

Another aspect was the collaboration between programmers and testers in both examples in order to automate the given examples. In the airport example, Tony paired with Alex on the automation. In the second example, we switched our thinking hats between test generation and design thinking from time to time to reach similar results.

Finally, literal automation serves also the purpose of representing the business domain in your tests. In fact, in the second example we saw how the traffic lights were first represented in the tests, and how the tests drove the domain model code from there.

Around 2010 I heard the term *domain-specific test language* for the first time. My first reaction was that there shouldn't be a discrepancy between the domain language that is used in your code and the one used in your tests at all. Sometimes— for example, in a legacy code system—you have no other choice but to keep the two separated when you begin your ATDD journey. Over time, though, you should unify the two into a single ubiquitous language used in your project. If you keep the two separated, you are growing and fostering miscommunication with your project stakeholders. One way to achieve this is to drive the domain code directly from your examples.

Let's take a closer look on these three aspects: Agile- and ATDD-friendly test automation, collaboration between programmers and testers, and finally how to discover the domain and a sufficient and appropriate domain model from your examples.

Use Friendly Automation

I heard the term *ATDD-friendly test automation* for the first time when I attended a tutorial on ATDD held by Elisabeth Hendrickson in 2009. It indicates that there are test automation tools available to support ATDD and literal automation.

One piece of advice at this point: Although we will dive into a tool discussion here, ATDD really is not about tooling; ATDD is an approach that can be used with many tools. If you implement a tool, you will get an implementation of that tool, but not an application of a working approach. A tool is not a test strategy [KBP01].

That said, let your team make the decision about the tool. There are multiple considerations in picking the right tool for your approach. The programming language used might play a role in your decision as well as readability concerns of your Product Owner or on-site customer. Depending on the degree your whole team, including programmers, testers, and business representatives, will work with the tool, you will prefer different aspects in the software.

As of this writing, there is a variety of test automation tools that support ATDD in diverse ways. Keywords, data-driven tests, and table structures all provide a ground to get started with ATDD. Some prefer the ability to automate via natural language, so that you can keep your examples readable like a document. Other prefer table structures or tests expressed in text files with a certain structure. Over time, though, all these features of the different tools started to influence the other frameworks as well, so that you can now work with either framework while still getting most benefit from the other frameworks around.

Part of this success comes from the OpenSource community. With the source code available for the major acceptance test frameworks around, new features and bugfixes are released timely. If you have an issue with one of the tools, you can usually file a question to one of the supplier's mailing lists or contact its support team. Most of the time you will get a helpful response within a day.

In the examples we already saw two such tools. Cucumber is a Ruby-based framework favoring tests in a behavior-driven development style. There are ports available for Java, Groovy, Scala, Clojure, and .NET, so that you can hook up your code with any of these languages. For more on Cucumber, see Appendix A and The Secret Ninja Cucumber Scrolls [dFAdF10].

The second example dealt with FitNesse. FitNesse is an acceptance test framework built in Java. It supports two test systems using either FIT and FitLibrary or SLiM. There are ports available for Java, .NET, Ruby, Python, and PHP. Since FitNesse is based upon a wiki, I found it suits distributed teams quite well. FitNesse itself is covered in more depth in Appendix B.

Other frameworks include Robot Framework, Concordion, JBehave, but also commercial ones such as Twist or Green Pepper. New frameworks may also be released in the next few years. These new tools might overcome some of the short-comings in the existing tools and reshape the tool landscape.

What all these tools have in common is an easy way to write text to express your requirements. Cucumber favors a Given-When-Then style, FitNesse has a table structure, and Robot Framework uses keywords. We saw examples of both styles in the examples.

What makes these tools friendly to ATDD is their ability to automate the examples given in a particular form with the usage of some code. The Cucumber steps use pattern matching with regular expression to decide which code to execute. For FitNesse with SLiM code, functions are called by convention. This creates a separation of concerns between the application that is tested and the textual representation of the tests.

When you use ATDD, you can derive the examples that you will test before writing a single line of code. Since the tools provide full test data separation from your application, you can grow the application alongside with the test examples, or even let your examples drive your implementation as we saw in the traffic lights example.

This separation of concerns between test data and application under test is the key to ATDD- and Agile-friendly test automation. When you adapt the ATDD approach, other tools will get in your way of a successful implementation. Test data separation is not a sufficient demand but a necessary one for a successful ATDD implementation.

Collaborate on Automation

Test automation is software development. Many experts have claimed this for decades. More interestingly, teams still fail to keep this in mind and end up completely lost with their test automation, eventually abandoning all their efforts for test automation at all. There is more to this particular topic, enough for me to include a separate chapter on test automation (see Chapter 12).

This section focuses on the collaboration part of test automation. As we saw in the airport example, tester Tony paired with Alex the test automation expert. Before that, Tony worked as far as he could on his own. When he got stuck completely, he knew he had to seek help.

One question that comes up in almost every class I teach on ATDD is the question whether the focus on test automation means that testers need to program. Many testers dropped out of programming because they did not feel passionate enough about programming. This sometimes leaves people with the impression that they are rather bad at programming.[1] Confronting them with ATDD can make them scared enough to resist the approach at all.

There is no need for testers to be afraid of ATDD. A focus on test automation does not mean that testers cannot collaborate with a programmer for test automation success. In fact, most programmers I paired with on test automation were more than eager to find out more about some of my skills as a tester as well. On the other hand, I learned new things about how an application was implemented as well as software design. Pairing on test automation is a win-win situation for the programmer and the tester.

When taking a closer look on the ATDD-friendly test automation frameworks, the frameworks decouple the tests from the tested application by introducing a mediation layer of code between these two aspects. In most teams starting with ATDD, testers maintain the test data while programmers are responsible for the system under test. But who should write the mediation code between these two aspects?

If the tester writes and maintains all the code that translates test examples to system calls in the application, then changes to the application might be overlooked if the programmer forgets to tell the tester. Once I worked with a company that

1. Some testers stated this as their self-perception. However, in most cases I do not agree with this.

had a separate testing department. The testers in that department were responsible for automating the tests on their own. Lack of communication forced a great deal of test automation rework.

On the other hand, if the programmer who maintains the portion of the application also writes the glue code to hook up the tests, changes in the application and the glue code may result in failing tests that were not adapted.

For both scenarios, the programmer and the tester have to communicate with each other. This is the lowest level of collaboration for test automation. I'd also claim that your team is not a team if it isn't communicating most of the time with each other. An informative workspace with Information Radiators [Coc06] can help with that. For example, you can put a pairing matrix on your taskboard if you experience a lack of collaboration between programmers and testers.

If you want better results with your test automation efforts, then programmers and testers should work closely together. In the best case they work on the glue code together side by side in a pair programming setup. The amount of information sharing in such a setting is immense enough that experienced pair programmers claim that pair programming yields a more than doubled productivity for the pair. This has been also my experience, although I don't have hard numbers on that.

Bringing both perspectives of the development project together at one desk to deal with the automation of part of the application also serves the purpose of exchange between the two specialists. The programmer learns a bit about testing and how the tester derives new test cases from the available information. The tester, on the other hand, learns more about programming, test-driven development, and can help the programmer to write maintainable code that the tester also understands.

Collaboration is a double-win situation for the whole project. Concerns about initial specialists in your team may be smoothed out through collaboration. Collaborating on test automation enables your team to implement collective test ownership, as Elisabeth Hendrickson calls it. With collective test ownership your whole team is empowered to write new tests and work on the automation code. This helps team members to cover for each other if progress is behind schedule. As a side effect, you will also get automated tests and a shared understanding of your test code and your tests.

Collaboration can come in many forms. As a minimum, testers and programmers should communicate about the glue code. Ideally, though, programmers and testers work together on critical parts of the automation code. The drawbacks of no collaboration at all are silo walls between programmers and testers, and in the worst case misunderstanding of the whole application. This can, in fact, destroy all your efforts for team building. By all means, I would rather avoid such a dysfunctional team.

Discover the Domain

In the traffic lights example we saw how to drive the domain code from the starting point of the tests. While driving the domain code, we also discovered some aspects about the domain itself. For example, the controller and the validator for valid light state combinations were not part of our initial design. The code we wrote in order to test the traffic lights motivated those concepts.

All our efforts as a software industry with domain-specific languages and behavior-driven development aside, there is a gap between the domain where our applications run and the domain model that is found in our code base. In our domain model we mostly add classes and constructs that are not existent in the real domain.

The Swedish Army has the following dictum [GW89]:

> When the map and the territory don't agree, always believe the territory.

Considering our domain model a map of the domain, if our domain model and our domain disagree, we should rather stick to the concepts in the domain, not the model.

On the other hand, as Michael Bolton put it,

> When you're lost, any old map will do.

This means that it is OK to get lost with your domain model from time to time, as long as you keep yourself in the position to adapt to the territory that you will find. You should work on the flexibility of your tests as well as the flexibility of your code. As long as you can adapt your code and your tests to the discoveries in the domain, you will be fine.

Tests and examples can guide our efforts to derive the domain model from the domain. They help us translate the real-world concepts and discover our model needs beyond them. Tests can help to elucidate missing elements in your domain model and code. Like the validator and the controller in the traffic lights example, these may not exist in the real world, but help to model the domain in the programming code.

As we saw in the traffic lights example, this technique works best if your programmers and testers work on the domain code and the automation code together. Not all teams work in this way. Driving the domain design and code from the outside-in does work poorly in these situations. Most teams starting with ATDD will not get this benefit right from the start. That's why I consider this an advanced technique.

Prerequisites to this are a close collaboration between programmers and testers. Ideally, programmers know and maintain all the test examples together with the testers. In this case, they can choose to drive the domain code outside in if they get stuck on the design without it. Ideally, though, I would aim to work outside-in all the time.

Another prerequisite for outside-in development is some experience. Experience can be gained over time by applying it more and more and learning from it. You might not see how to drive your code from the outside right from the beginning, but you should push yourself forward to do this. Whenever you see a possibility to drive your code, take it.

If you want to reconsider your position on outside-in development, ask yourself, whether there are other possibilities other than the ones you see right now. Remember the Rule of Three interpretations, as Jerry Weinberg coined it [Wei93]. If you can't think of three different approaches to drive your code, you haven't thought enough about the problem—or you didn't ask yourself the crucial questions on problem definitions: What is the problem?; Who has it?; Who should fix it?

Don't decide that you can't drive your code and your domain model from the outside-in until you have found at least three different ways to do it. At least three means that you might easily find five possibilities. Then you pick the one that looks most promising to you while still considering the constraint to drive the code from the outside-in. If you thought about three different possibilities to write that code, and still see no way to drive it outside-in, write it in the most promising way. Over time your experience with outside-in development will grow, and you will see more opportunities. Keep in mind that code is not cast in stone, and today's integrated development environments (IDEs) provide a multitude of ways to restructure and rewrite your code later.

Summary

When you automate your examples, there are a few points to watch out for. First, make sure that you use the right tool to do it. Involve your whole team into that decision, because potentially everyone else has to work with it at some point in the future. Second, you want to avoid barriers for anyone on your team to this and also make sure that the tool serves your process, and not the other way around.

With tooling barriers removed, you should also be able to collaborate on automation. A tester can benefit from design knowledge of programmers, and programmers can benefit from the testing knowledge from the tester. As a side-effect this will also help to spread the tacit knowledge in the heads of your team, thereby helping you reach a common understanding of the problem you are solving for your customer.

Outside-in development can help with this, too. If the application domain code reflects your common understanding, then you might be able to have your customer at least read and understand your code. If you use your acceptance tests to discover the domain you are dealing with, you can drive your application, design, and architecture in completely different directions. This helps building applications that are easy to maintain in the long-run.

Chapter 12
Test Cleanly

Working tests are the most precious asset in any software development project. They not only show that your system is still useful in some way, but they also document what the system does—and you can check that with the press of a button if you have automated your tests.

Since working tests are so valuable to your development project, you should keep them working under all circumstances—or make an informed decision to get rid of them. With today's version control systems it's not a shame to throw away things that you no longer need. In fact, it gives you some relief. Teams not only report that fewer tests provide them with more flexibility (see [Adz11]), but also relieves some of the burden to our brains [Hun08].

You may argue that a good organization of test cases helps you do that, too. But up to which point do you want to keep all of your tests? A few years back I was part of a project for a customer in Brazil where the testers automated all tests that came to mind. Brazil has a tax system that allows each of the twenty-seven states to apply a different tax system. In our system our programmers had to configure one subset for each tax system.

The first shot of automated tests consisted of roughly 300 times 27 tax variations test cases. The overall test suite took more than two days to execute in a single run. Despite all the efforts put into that code for automation and the tests themselves, that test automation was completely worthless at the time I entered the project.

The automated tests did not provide any useful answer on any update of the software in a timely manner. This resulted in business decisions being made without reference to the test outcomes that turned up two days later. The whole test automation effort had painted itself into the corner.

So, what did we do to get the automation back under control? We had to throw away test cases. We analyzed the approach to generate each product and sought the risks that came with that approach. Then we tackled those risks rather than all the risks that could have happened with any approach. By doing that we were able to throw out the majority of the test cases altogether. Now, I would apply a pairwise approach to reduce the number of test cases (see Chapter 9, "Pairwise Testing" and [HK11]).

The underlying problem was that the tests were not maintained. They were not clean, but instead contained a lot of buzz that burdened the testing team. The business stakeholders made decisions that overruled any test outcome, and finally the bugs that backfired burdened the programmers as well, because they had to deal with the rework.

All of this can be avoided if you keep an eye on your automated tests and avoid tests becoming broken windows. The Broken Window Rule [HT99] is based on an observation from uninhabited houses. Nothing might happen for quite some time to these houses once the last habitant left. But once the first unrepaired broken window shows up, more and more windows get broken. The same happens to our code base as well as to our entire test base.

For your code base, there are very good books on the topic. For example, you may consider *Clean Code* [Mar08a] by Robert Martin, or *Refactoring to Patterns* [Ker04] by Joshua Kerievsky. For test code you might consider *xUnit Test Patterns* [Mes07] by Gerard Meszaros, which should give you a good start. Some of these apply also quite well to acceptance tests.

Over the years I found three main lessons from all the literature on the topic. First of all, test automation is software development. This implies that I have to use proper software development practices to develop my test automation, and that I also need to test my test automation code. Second, your tests will start to smell bad at one point or the other. At this point, it pays to follow this smell and seek opportunities to improve not only the software but also the software development process that created that smell. Last, but not least, one of the most hurtful things missing in software test automation at the time of this writing is refactoring tools that not only change your test automation code, but also your tests. I will provide some clues to the patterns I have seen so far in the different frameworks that probably can be automated.

Develop Test Automation

One of the main advantages of incremental and iterative software development is that it's hard for ever-larger systems to anticipate all requirements and functions up front. Previously, software was developed with the mindset that all the requirements for the next version of the software can be gathered before any coding starts, only to find that adapting to the changes in the business process was necessary in the meantime, as well as patching your system to adapt to them.

Iterative and incremental development builds upon existing features. The idea is to start with the most basic version of the feature that you can imagine. When you are done implementing this version, you add the next increment to refine it. For example, you might start with a Walking Skeleton (see [Coc06]) and start to add more flesh to it later. You might leave out validation code that rejects invalid input values to the system. By building the most valuable cut through the software system first, then dealing with the special cases, incremental development becomes a success.

The iterative and incremental approach to test automation also works for your glue code for the textual representation of your examples and the system under test. In the airport example we saw how Tony and Alex made the first test pass, then automated one example after the other. Later, Tony automated incrementally from that basis by adding the remaining parking lots to the code.

The key to this basis is a design that is flexible in the dimension that you will extend to later. After being able to input different starting and ending parking times, selecting the proper parking lot was a no-brainer. Design decisions influence the flexibility of the test automation code. In the airport parking lot example, the problem was easy. Alex and Tony could easily foresee design decisions for the future, and therefore also end up with a flexible design approach.

On real projects things often turn out way more ugly than this simple example. Even for the traffic lights example, things started out to be more complicated than we might have anticipated. On more complex domains, it pays therefore to focus on the most basic flow through the system first, then continue from this base camp.

When I worked at a company on a replacement for its test automation system, we had many business use cases that we would have to automate in the replacement system. We could have started with a long analysis, laid out the plan for the new design, and implemented everything we knew. Instead, we analyzed all the use cases and their flow for likelihood of failures and their impact on the business. Then we assigned each of the business use cases a criticality. We started with the most critical use cases in our new test automation approach as it gave us the biggest return on investment quickly. Eighteen weeks later we found ourselves finished with the transition. Having dealt with the biggest problems first, it was very easy to replace the tests for the use cases with lower business criticality. Indeed, the use cases we automated first addressed many risks that allowed us to build a basis for the other use cases later.

One major lesson is to avoid putting all the logic in one large glue code class. In FIT, for example, you can decide to put translation code between the business objects such as money (a double plus a currency) directly into the Fixture class.

You can also add large behavior flows like adding an account with an address in your class directly. This approach is as bad as putting all the business logic in the GUI classes of your application.

First of all, you create a code base that is hard to test automatically through unit tests on its own. The object model of your test code lacks the existence of commonly used domain objects like money and an AccountCreator. Eventually, your team members will lack an understanding of how to deal with the code that you created and keep reinventing the wheel. In the worst case, you end up with a large test support code base that is copied and pasted together. At this point you already have shot yourself in the foot with your test automation efforts as new features become harder and harder to automate based on that.

If you build your support code in components, you create independent helpers that you can include or extend in the future. In the traffic lights example we extracted the concept of a CrossingController as a component. Although we actually put it in our domain model in the end, the crossing controller is an example of such an independent component.

As we saw later, there is another advantage to building small components for your test automation support code. Independent components are easier to unit test in themselves. Since test automation is software development, you should consider unit testing more complex flows through the support code on its own. As I mentioned in Chapter 9, I once heard from a team where test-driving the test automation code led to a major increase (10-15%) in test coverage in the whole system. If you find yourself adding one `if` or `switch` statement after another, consider refactoring your code to a more object-oriented structure such as a strategy pattern [GHJV94] or an independent component.

Listen to the Tests

Unit tests can teach you a lot about the design of your classes [FP09]. If the unit tests are awkward to write—and read for that matter—they may give you hints to a missing concept in your design.

From my experience, this does not only hold for unit tests, but also for acceptance tests. If you need a lot of support code—especially complicated with many nested `if`s—this implies a missing concept either in your application or in your support code. If you have built your acceptance criteria on business examples, it's most likely that your application is missing a domain concept.

We saw an example of this with the traffic lights example. There we took the tests and the support code to motivate the domain concepts in the code. This is one way to listen to your tests and drive your implementation from these.

But some teams don't give access to the production code and domain model to their testers. At this point it becomes absolutely necessary to have collaboration between testers and programmers in place. If testers realize problems with long and hard-to-read tests, but can't do a thing about them, then the code base will start to degenerate quickly.

On the other hand, if testers can provide the programmers the feedback that something is wrong based on what they see happening to the tests, then the programmers might become aware of a problem in the code and come up with creative solutions together with the testers.

Ideally, you worked completely from the outside in to your code base. The probability, then, is small that you will end up with long tests or hard-to-read examples. I found myself painted into the corner more often if I retrofitted acceptance-level tests to already existing code. One of the major drawbacks was that it was inconvenient or even awkward to hook the tests up, since I hadn't anticipated all necessary entry points for end-to-end tests. If you work from the outside in, you will have to create all the hooks by definition.

Listening to your tests works on three different levels if you apply ATDD. First, you can listen to your examples. If they end up long, and rather reflect a complete flow through the system with many steps, then they indicate a missing abstraction between the business focus and the technical implementation details.

Consider an inlined example for the airport example in Listing 12.1. This test consist of keywords from the Selenium library in Robot Framework. It tests the condition that we parked a car in the Economy Parking lot for one day, 23 hours, and 11 minutes. There are several flaws to this example. The most prevalent one is that we will get a headache once we try to maintain this in the longer run. It does not express its intention. The text is too verbose. We should clearly refactor this test.

Listing 12.1 A verbose example for the airport parking lot calculator

```
1 Basic Test
2     Open Browser  http://www.shino.de/parkcalc/  firefox
3     Set Selenium Speed  0
4     Title Should Be  Parking Calculator
5     Select From List  Lot  Economy Parking
6     Input Text  EntryTime  01:23
7     Select Radio Button  EntryTimeAMPM  AM
8     Input Text  EntryDate  02/28/2000
9     Input Text  ExitTime  12:34
```

```
10      Select Radio Button  ExitTimeAMPM   AM
11      Input Text  ExitDate  03/01/2000
12      Click Button   Submit
13      Page Should Contain   (1 Days, 23 Hours, 11 Minutes)
14      [Teardown]   Close Browser
```

Contrast this with the examples for economy parking that Tony, Phyllis, and Bill identified in the airport example (see Listing 12.2).

Listing 12.2 The Economy Parking Lot automated examples (reprint from Listing 3.4)

```
1  Feature: Economy Parking feature
2    The parking lot calculator can calculate costs for Economy
       parking.
3
4    Scenario Outline: Calculate Economy Parking Cost
5      When I park my car in the Economy Parking Lot for <parking
         duration>
6      Then I will have to pay <parking costs>
7
8    Examples:
9    | parking duration      | parking costs |
10   | 30 minutes            | $ 2.00        |
11   | 1 hour                | $ 2.00        |
12   | 4 hours               | $ 8.00        |
13   | 5 hours               | $ 9.00        |
14   | 6 hours               | $ 9.00        |
15   | 24 hours              | $ 9.00        |
16   | one day, one hour     | $ 11.00       |
17   | one day, three hours| $ 15.00       |
18   | one day, five hours   | $ 18.00       |
19   | six days              | $ 54.00       |
20   | six days, one hour    | $ 54.00       |
21   | seven days            | $ 54.00       |
22   | one week, two days    | $ 72.00       |
23   | three weeks           | $ 162.00      |
```

One way to solve this is to create an abstraction layer in a keyword-driven manner. Tony did this in the airport example when he introduced the examples based upon the business requirements automatically. But you may also discover the necessity for such a layer later. Then you should come up with additional scenarios like we did in the traffic light example for the invalid light state combinations in the first crossing controller. There we added the abstraction of an invalid state. In retrospect what led us there was the notion that our table had many repeated entries for the invalid light states, which led to yellow blinking lights. This was an example of listening to the tests when your examples become longer and redundant.

Another way to solve the problem of long tests is to introduce domain concepts in the support code or domain code. We saw this in the traffic lights example when we introduced the domain concept of a light state to the domain code based upon our acceptance tests. Later we found out about the necessity for a state validator based upon our acceptance tests for a crossing.

Once I worked on a project where we had to deal with different types of accounts. These could have multiple child accounts together with different subscriptions. Our first approach in test automation there was to describe the whole hierarchy for the test we needed. Once we had automated most business flows in this manner, we eventually realized that this was hard to maintain in the long term.

At that point, the tests told us that we worked on the wrong level of abstraction as well. By sitting together with the business side we came up with the concept of different tariff structures expressed in the test examples. Instead of an account hierarchy with one top-level and one subscription account with product XYZ, we called the whole hierarchy branch a subscription in tariff XYZ and hid the implicated selling of different products to the subscriber in that term. See Listing 12.3 for an example of such a table.

Listing 12.3 A setup table preparing three different account hierarchies with different tariffs and products hidden in the back

```
1 !|Account Creator                      |
2 |account name    |tariff               |
3 |Peter Prepaid   |Prepaid Basic 50     |
4 |Paul Postpaid   |Postpaid Business 100|
5 |Claus Convergent|Convergent Family 150|
```

In that project we as testers didn't have access to the source code, so we put the responsibility for selling the products into the support code for our tests. We created a lookup for different business tariff names and applied several operations on a standard account for each tariff. When we finished, we noticed that we had thrown out accidental complexity from the test examples into the support code, thereby making the tests easier to handle and maintain.

The second way to listen to your tests is by looking at the glue or the support code. In the traffic lights example we saw this happening when we identified the need for an enumeration of light states. The glue code told us, that there were going to be multiple `if-then-else` constructs adding unnecessary complexity to the glue code.

The glue code there really told us that we needed a higher-level concept. Our examples were easy to read and quite short at that point in time. But our code wasn't. That's where listening to the glue code rather than the examples helped us make the decision to come up with the concept of a `LightState`.

At times your support code may be hard to handle. At this point, it is really telling you that it's lacking some sort of concept. At this point you should stop, reflect on your code, and see if you can see that new concept arising. If you can't, give it some more time. If you see the missing concept lurking in the code, then try to extract it.

Finally, there is a third way to listen to your tests. This way applies if you drive your test automation code using test-driven development. Your unit tests might be hard to write. At this point all the lessons from Steve Freeman and Nat Pryce in *Growing Object-oriented Software Guided by Tests* [FP09] apply. Suffice it to say that you listen similarly to your unit tests as you listen to your acceptance tests. Still, I whole-heartedly recommend Freeman's and Pryce's book if you still want to dig deeper.

Refactor Tests

At the time of this writing, one of the final frontiers for automating your tests is the ability to restructure existing tests. I hope to see some advancement in the years to come. There are already some tools available that close the gap, but so far I have seen only add-ons to existing tools to do that.

In programming, refactoring code refers to changing the internal structure of the code, but not changing the functionality or what it does [FBB+99]. While the internals to the code structure are changed, the functionality is preserved.

Initially, refactorings were small steps combined such as renaming a method or extracting a variable. Over time, by combining several such lower-level refactorings, more complex ones came to life. For example, Extract Superclass is a higher level refactoring.

A few years back, integrated development environments (IDEs) didn't come with refactoring support. Back in those days, refactoring was a time-consuming activity that could break the whole code base. For Smalltalk, automated refactoring tools existed, but not for Java or C++. Automated refactorings are safer than following the steps by hand, since they are just executed if they can preserve the previous functionality.

Now, there is nearly no IDE without automated refactoring support. Refactorings such as changing the name of a class or extracting a method from a code snippet are easy to access and safe to use now and are well-used among programmers.

Unfortunately, Agile-friendly test automation tools mostly lack refactoring support for your tests. While easy renaming, such as changing the color red to blue, may be achieved with a shell script using, for example, sed and regular expressions, more complex changes like the exchange of two columns in a table or extending a table by one column are tedious manual tasks.

ReFit from Johannes Link[1] is one of the add-on tools that I would like to see incorporated into the acceptance test frameworks around today. It provides the ability to search and replace in existing data as well as restructure the existing examples to some degree. With an integrated development environment for acceptance tests, we could perhaps overcome this shortcoming as well, but my experience with such IDEs for testers has been that they come with even more payload than necessary.

Most of the tools that claim to be test automation super tools usually follow this pattern:

- They come with a set of standard functions that someone requested, i.e., database queries.
- They come with some graphical representation of the examples.
- They are bundled with a license model that forces companies to buy just enough licenses for their testers, but not the programmers.

The first shortcoming results in a high degree of functions available to testers. Unfortunately, this also may lead to testers using these lower-level functions directly in the tests. At that point, the tests become coupled to how the application is implemented rather than abstracted from that and focusing on the business goals.

The second shortcoming results in a higher complexity for refactoring or updating your tests. Eventually, you will have to redraw all the tiny little graphics that make working in these IDEs very convenient. But the degree of test maintenance necessary to change anything can pretty much blow any project.

---

1. http://johanneslink.net/projects/refit.jsp

The last shortcoming results in poor collaboration in the team. Since programmers do have access to IDEs, they won't run the functional acceptance tests before checking in any code. This will, of course, lengthen the feedback loop for them in case they break something. When they have moved on to the next task, once you find a bug in their changes, they will have a hard time remembering what they did there in first place.

Regarding refactoring of your tests, the second argument is a showstopper for graphical tools. They might provide an interface that lets you work without any programming knowledge. But this also means that your programmers will not adapt their interfaces to your tests when they execute an automated refactoring in their IDE. This also means that you will have a lot of manual work if you need to update something. Although programmers nowadays come with some abstraction layers on their own to decouple changes in the application from changes in the test examples, the flexibility to refactor your tests to an additional data set is still based on other tools like a spreadsheet program.

Getting back to Agile-friendly test automation tools, all of the tools available today lack the ability to easily restructure the examples. I see great potential in such a feature, because it would simplify very tedious tasks for us testers in the long run, once a new feature makes massive changes to previously existing tests necessary.

In the meantime, I would like to describe two refactorings that I found convenient. These refer back to similar refactorings for source code, and I think the two build a basis for more advanced refactorings of tests in the future.

Extract Variable

The first refactoring in that list is to extract a variable. A variable represents a placeholder, the convenient use of repeated values. For example, we might extract the value for yellow blink into a variable in the traffic lights example. We can then give this variable the name invalid configuration and can easily replace a bunch of occurrences of yellow blink by changing just the contents of the variable.

You will find this refactoring necessary if you can foresee a lot of changes in a particular dimension. While the change for an invalid combination might seem unlikely in the traffic lights example, if you consider shipping our traffic lights system to different countries where different configurations for invalid states might exist, you will see that this prepares the tests for configurability of the application. If this is a future evolution point of the system, we can incorporate this right from the start.

If you already have tests and want to extract a variable from the existing data, here is a sequence I often use.

1. Find the value that you would like to store in a variable.

2. Define the variable and fill it with the desired value. Run your tests so that you see any unwanted changes, such as an already existing variable with the same name.

3. Replace the first occurrence of the value with the newly defined variable. Run your tests to see that you didn't break anything.

4. For each additional occurrence repeat the previous step. After each change run your tests.

Extract Keyword

In case I see one step being used in several tests, I consider extracting a keyword so that my tests become easier to read. In a source code context, this refactoring is similar to extracting a method from a code snipplet.

In the traffic lights example we saw this nearly happen when we introduced the concept of an invalid light state keyword (Listing 12.4 repeats the examples). We combined multiple steps in the test table to create a new keyword for this commonly used flow. Other uses may be to log into the system by entering a username and a password. The login function might turn out as a function that most tests need to execute at some point.

Listing 12.4 Extracted keyword for invalid light state combinations (repeated from Listing 7.15)

```
1  ...
2  !2 Invalid combinations
3
4  !|scenario          |invalid combination|firstLight||secondLight|
5  |set first light |@firstLight                                  |
6  |set second light|@secondLight                                 |
7  |execute                                                       |
8  |check            |first light        |yellow blink            |
9  |check            |second light       |yellow blink            |
10
11 !|script|FirstLightSwitchingCrossingController|
12
13 !|invalid combination    |
14 |firstLight   |secondLight|
15 |green        |red, yellow|
```

```
16 |green        |green       |
17 |green        |yellow      |
18 |yellow       |red, yellow|
19 |yellow       |green       |
20 |yellow       |yellow      |
21 |red, yellow |red, yellow|
22 |red, yellow |green       |
23 |red, yellow |yellow      |
24 |red          |red, yellow|
25 |red          |green       |
26 |red          |yellow      |
27 |yellow blink|red         |
28 |yellow blink|red, yellow|
29 |yellow blink|green       |
30 |yellow blink|yellow      |
```

Compared to variables, keywords provide the ability to take parameters. At that point you really create a function with no return value if you extract a keyword.

I worked with systems where we created multiple levels of keywords with higher-level keywords covering higher-level concepts being glued together to an even more higher-level concept and lower-level keywords, which some higher-level keywords could use. There is a drawback to too many levels of keywords. Since you don't have the ability to easily dive into the keyword hierarchy nowadays, it might become awkward to create, find, and maintain too many levels of keywords.

Here are the steps I usually take to extract a keyword from an existing example.

1. Identify the flow you would like to name more conveniently.
2. Create a new keyword covering all the parameters that you will need. Run your tests to notice side effects of redundant keywords.
3. Replace the first occurrence of the flow with your new keyword, passing all necessary parameters. Run your tests to check that you didn't break anything.
4. Repeat the previous step for each occurrence of the flow. Run your tests after each change.

Summary

In order to build clean tests, you have to treat test automation as software development. That means to incorporate any development practices that you also apply to your production code. That includes not only to unit test your test automation code, but also to refactor it. Finally, keep decoupled designs and architectures in mind when building your mediation code.

At times you will find out that a particular test is hard to write, or hard to automate. This is a case where you should listen to your tests, and seek the problem in how you build your application so far. Use the information that your tests reveal to change the problem in your code.

If you run into the situation that something in the domain changes, then you will face the struggle that you have to change a large number of tests. For source code, the term refactoring refers to structural changes of the code that do not change anything in the behavior of the program. In order to build and maintain your tests cleanly, we will need tool support for basic refactorings. We have seen two here: extract a keyword and extract a variable. I expect more to be discovered in the near future.

Chapter 13

Successful ATDD

This concludes our journey into acceptance test-driven development, specification by example, or agile acceptance testing. In order to get started with your own business level examples, try identifying acceptance criteria in one of the formats that we worked through. Don't spend much time on finding the correct format in your case. Adopting a new approach means that you will have to learn new things, play around with some of the concepts, and see what works for you and what does not. Do not let yourself become paralyzed by the many options you can choose. Get started on one particular business flow and start to grow your acceptance tests from that.

I am assuming that you are currently not working with ATDD here, and that you are working on a product that already exists to some degree. You need to retrofit some acceptance tests to the already existing parts. This probably will mean that you have to negotiate with your customer representative how to set the necessary time for this aside. To get the first prototype started, you may want to timebox your efforts. At one client we were charged with creating a prototype for an SWT-based application. I was unfamiliar with the driver for SWT application—we chose SWTBot. We took half a day pairing together to find out how to hook up SWTBot to the SWT application. We had picked a flow through the system that seemed complex enough to have a first prototype, but not impossible to us at that time.

We started with a straightforward approach. We basically had everything in one single big test function when we ran the first test. From that we started to refactor the test code so that it became modular and maintainable in the long run. We took another half day one sprint later to get this approach from JUnit to FitNesse. At that point we had a first step toward our safety-net of acceptance tests.

Where you start with the first set of acceptance tests does not matter much. You should strive for very common business scenarios. At one company we did a risk analysis for the business use cases and based our starting points on the most risky use cases as well as the ones that were most often executed. This ensured that we started on the right foot and could also use the first set of tests and automation code as a baseline for the other use cases.

While becoming more and more familiar and experienced with the approach that you picked, you should also make sure to speak with your business representative about the requirements. Try to find a way to note the examples in the structures you are familiar with. Use the tables to communicate with your business representative and show him or her the end results once you automated these examples.

Remember to include the right persons at the right time in your specification workshops. Refrain from inviting too many people, but also make sure you have the right people at the table. You should also make sure to pick the right moment. If your product owner in Scrum is busy accepting or rejecting the results of your sprint in the final two days, it might not be a good time to discuss the requirements for the next sprint—for your product owner as well as for your team.

When you automated the first few examples, you should also strive to incorporate them into your continuous integration system. Only if your automated tests are executed regularly without thinking about it do they serve you any purpose. For most tools there are plug-ins for commonly used CI systems available. If not, then there is probably a team that already faced a similar situation as you do. Ask on official web or technical sites for support. Maybe the maintainers of the tool also know a way to incorporate the results for your particular CI system.

As your base of automated tests grows and grows, make sure you have a safety net in place for them as well. Over time you may want to change the organization of your tests to reflect your understanding of the domain. In one company we started with the organization based upon use cases. Over time we saw that changes were coming in based upon certain tariff models. We reorganized our tests around different tariff models rather than the business use cases. Whatever the organization you pick first, it will not be a problem to change it later.

Also keep an eye on your automation code base. Make sure to unit test the code you write to automate the tests. This may become tricky in case you use a lot of keywords or scenario tables, because these are usually not unit testable.

Make sure you refactor your code. Regardless of whether you are in a position to grow domain objects out of your automation code, you should strive to encapsulate domain concepts in their own objects. For webpages this might mean coming up with page objects for each webpage, or you might deal with domain objects like money, accounts, users, and receipts. Keeping these concepts in their own classes helps you to make extensions later more easily, and thereby avoiding the test automation maintenance hell that so many teams face.

Over time you may also want to rewrite some of your earlier examples when you see the liabilities of your first steps. Don't skimp in the effort to change them now before the project grows more complex. The temptation to simply copy and paste this example, change some data, and then check in your results is great. Do not go there. Instead, think about how you might incorporate your new example in a way that it will be easier to come up with additional examples later. You might want to express your tests in a tabular format, or you might seek a new abstraction layer in your examples. Copy and pasting might be easy, but treat it as a symptom to a problem in your code base.

To get started, keep in mind trying out some approach for a limited time, reflecting on your current experiences with it, and adapting. You might speculate a lot about a better approach. Try to get started instead, and solve the problems that you might face when you actually run into them. Track how the tiny changes you actually make contribute to larger improvements over time. I believe this is a recipe for successful approaches—not only considering ATDD, but software development in general.

Appendix A
Cucumber

In this appendix we will give a brief introduction to Cucumber. For a more in-depth introduction check *The RSpec book* [CAH+10], the *Secret Ninja Cucumber Scrolls* [dFAdF10], or the Cucumber website at http://cukes.info. Both books handle more advanced topics such as setup and teardown mechanisms and organization of your feature files.

Cucumber is a behavior-driven development (BDD) test automation tool. That means that you will need to describe your examples using the Given-When-Then format.

Cucumber is based upon Ruby. If you have Ruby installed, run the command `gem install cucumber` with administrator privileges, and wait for the installation to succeed. If the installation complains about missing dependencies, you may have to add the -y option to the gem command. In newer installations `gem` automatically derives the dependencies by default.

Feature Files

In order to get started, you need a feature file. A feature file describes the feature that you are about to implement in your application. A sample feature file consists of a feature line that names and describes the feature and one or several scenarios or scenario outlines. Each scenario or scenario outline consists of any number of Given-steps, one When-step, and one or multiple Then-steps.

The Given-steps might be left out. This is especially the case when you set up the system in a common set up inside the code, or if there is nothing special to get your application started. The When- and the Then-steps are mandatory in order to execute and test something in your application at all.

An example feature file is shown in Listing A.1.

Listing A.1 An example Cucumber feature file

```
1 Feature: Valet Parking feature
2   The parking lot calculator can calculate costs for Valet
      Parking.
3
```

```
 4   Scenario Outline: Calculate Valet Parking Cost
 5     When I park my car in the Valet Parking Lot for <parking
       duration>
 6     Then I will have to pay <parking costs>
 7
 8   Examples:
 9   | parking duration   | parking costs |
10   | 30 minutes         | $ 12.00       |
11   | 3 hours            | $ 12.00       |
12   | 5 hours            | $ 12.00       |
13   | 5 hours 1 minute   | $ 18.00       |
14   | 12 hours           | $ 18.00       |
15   | 24 hours           | $ 18.00       |
16   | 1 day 1 minute     | $ 36.00       |
17   | 3 days             | $ 54.00       |
18   | 1 week             | $ 126.00      |
```

Step Definitions

The next step when working from the outside in is to hook up the steps to some program code. These hooks are called step definitions in Cucumber language. They depend heavily on the programming language in use. In Ruby, which is the default for Cucumber, the step definitions consist of closures surrounded by appropriate pattern matches. Each Given-step is introduced by the Given keyword plus a regular expression that matches the feature file line. The When- and Then-steps are defined in a similar way. Listing A.2 shows an example of such a definition for the above feature file.

Listing A.2 The step definitions for the above feature file

```
1 When /^I park my car in the Valet Parking Lot for (.*)$/ do |
    duration|
2   $parkcalc.select('Valet Parking')
3   $parkcalc.enter_parking_duration(duration)
4 end
5
6 Then /^I will have to pay (.*)$/ do |price|
7   $parkcalc.parking_costs.should == price
8 end
```

Hook-up mechanisms for other programming languages are similar, although they make use of the language specific mechanisms like annotations in Java. If you would like to use a port to a different language, check the documentation for the actual syntax.

Production Code

At this point you can start developing the production system. In the airport example we used a mediation layer, which some people call page objects. It mediates the hooks to the actual implementation of the website. This appears to be a strategy most suitable for web applications. For non-web-UI code you will probably just start from the step definition code to drive all of your code.

Appendix B
FitNesse

This appendix gives a brief introduction to FitNesse—the acceptance test wiki. For a more in-depth material, check out the website at http://fitnesse.org. The book on *Fit for Developing Software* [MC05] covers also a bit of FitNesse, although the material is a bit dated. For example, it does not deal with the Simple List invocation Method (SLiM) tables, which Robert C. Martin introduced in 2008.

Figure B.1 shows the FitNesse architecture involving the two test systems—FIT and SLiM. The test cases are wiki pages organized in a hierarchical structure. FitNesse then either executes tests using the FIT client or the SLiM client. This is steered by defining a variable. You can redefine this variable inside the hierarchy thereby allowing you to mix FIT and SLiM tests—although all FIT tests will be executed separately from all the SLiM tests if you run the whole suite.

Behind the process boundary, the FIT client and the SLiM runner invoke different methods based on conventions. These methods then involve the system under test in order to drive the tests or to gather certain results in the system itself.

The older FIT system comes with a GPLv2 model and uses inheritance to mediate between the tests and the application. Thus, all your fixture code becomes effectively licensed under GPLv2. I'm not a lawyer, but some companies didn't like this licensing model, so Robert C. Martin came up with a test system that uses convention over inheritance. I will leave out the FIT discussion and focus on SLiM as the test system.

Wiki Structure

Wiki pages consist of a name in a camel-case format. A camel-case name for a page that deals with accounts reloading some balance could be AccountReloading. A camel cased name has at least two uppercase letters and no spaces.

Wiki pages in FitNesse can be nested into suites. You can use suites to combine parts of your system that belong together and should be tested together. FitNesse lets you execute the tests in a sub-suite in separation from the rest, while you can still execute all the tests from the top level or even a test at a leaf.

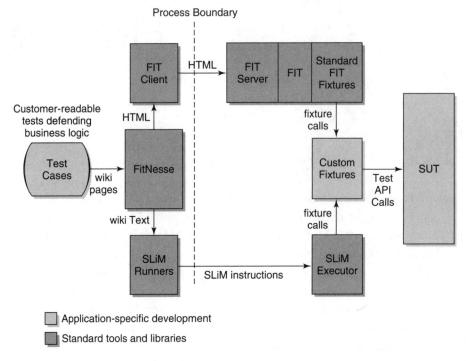

Figure B.1 The FitNesse architecture showing the two test systems

Wikis come in handy when you organize knowledge. Since you can link to other wiki pages, FitNesse let's you create your test examples together with your written documentation, and basically all other necessary information like common flows through your system.

SLiM Tables

There are some table structures that you can use in order to express examples for your application. The most convenient table is the decision table. It consists of input values to the system and outputs that are checked after executing some operation. Listing B.1 shows an example.

Listing B.1 A FitNesse SLiM decision table

```
1 !|Traffic Lights            |
2 |previous state|next state? |
3 |red           |red, yellow |
4 |red, yellow   |green       |
5 |green         |yellow      |
6 |yellow        |red         |
7 |invalid state |yellow blink|
```

For sets of values there are query tables. These become handy when you have collections of data to check in your system. For example, you might want to check a list of accounts that are in your system or fulfill a certain constraint for your test. In a query table you list all the objects on one line each. You can define multiple properties that will be checked. Listing B.2 shows an example query.

Listing B.2 A FitNesse SLiM query table

```
1 !|Query:Active Accounts         |
2 |account number|account name     |
3 |123           |John Doe         |
4 |42            |Jane Doe         |
5 |24141         |Luke Skywalker|
6 |51214         |Darth Vader    |
```

You can use decision tables and query tables together in a single test. Usually this means wrapping both in some execution plan together. This is where the script table comes into play. For decision tables you can leave out the checked outputs. The decision tables then become setup tables to create anything you need for your test. In a script table you then execute some action like working on a previously created account. In the end you may check the results of that operation in script instructions or query tables.

This format is similar to the Given-When-Then-format of the BDD approach we see in Cucumber. The setup table describe all the Givens, the script table action describes the When-step, and the Then-steps are checked by either script actions or by a query table.

This mechanism becomes more powerful when you use it in combination with scenario tables. Scenario tables let you extract common steps from script tables, which you need several times. You introduce a layer of higher-level abstractions with these scenario tables. It is similar to the keyword approach that Robot Framework (http://robotframework.org)—another Agile-friendly test automation tool—provides.

Support Code

Support code for the SLiM tables can be written in multiple languages. Java is the native one for FitNesse, but there are also SLiM ports to Ruby, Python, .NET, and PHP just to name a few. We will focus on Java here.

For decision tables, you have to implement a setter for each input column and provide a getter for each output column. The SLiM runner will automatically find the appropriate setter and getter based on the column name.

For query tables you have to return three nested lists of strings. The inner-most list represents individual cells containing the label of the header column and the particular cell data. These are combined for each line in the middle list. The outer-most list collects all the lists. It took me some time to get my head around this. Once you understand the clue, it becomes rather easy.

For script tables the name of the function that is called is constructed by camel casing the line. Parameters in each even column are forwarded to the function. A script table like the one in Listing B.3 would be translated to the method call `scriptWithSomeParameters(String value1, String value2)` at the class `ScriptTable`.

Listing B.3 A FitNesse SLiM script table

```
1  !|script|ScriptTable|
2  |script with|param1|some|param2|parameters|
```

For more in-depth material check out the FitNesse user guide and the tutorials from Brett Schuchert, which are linked on the main FitNesse entrance page.

Appendix C
Robot Framework

In this appendix I will give a brief introduction to Robot Framework. Robot Framework comes with fantastic documentation. Check out the user guide[1] if you seek more in-depth material. I especially found the documentation for the included libraries[2] helpful while working with Robot.

To get started with Robot you need Python. There is a Java implementation as well, which lets you write the glue code in native Java rather than Python. From the Python installation you can follow the installation instructions.[3] They are straightforward. After the installation, you will have a `pybot` or `jybot` executable depending on your actual Python installation. If you use Python, you will have `pybot`; if you use the Java-based Jython, you will have `jybot` in your path. I will concentrate on `pybot` in the following. If you use Jython, please substitute calls to `pybot` with `jybot` respectively.

Robot Framework can use test data from multiple data formats. There is HTML, tabulator-separated values, and plain text. In most cases I ended up using the plain text format because I find it the most readable. For plain text, you can also use multiple representations. There is the space separated format, the pipe and space separated format, and the restructured text format. I'll concentrate on the pipe and space separated format because it is the best format for printing. Refer to the user guide for the others.

Sections

In Robot Framework the test files use several sections. Metadata-like libraries of keywords you want to use in your tests are described in the Settings section of your test. Test cases are defined in the Test Cases section, and you can define custom keywords on your own in a section called Keywords. Finally, you can define variables in a section called Variables.

---

1. http://code.google.com/p/robotframework/wiki/UserGuide
2. http://code.google.com/p/robotframework/wiki/TestLibraries
3. http://code.google.com/p/robotframework/wiki/Installation

In the Settings section you may document your test cases, list setup and teardown keywords for your tests as well as for your suite, or load keywords from another text file. In Listing C.1 you can see such a settings section for tests in Robot Framework that I wrote for the parking lot calculator. In line 4 I use a file called `resource.txt`, which is similar to our `env.rb` that we saw in the first example using Cucumber.

Listing C.1 A Robot Framework settings section used for the airport parking lot calculator

```
1 ** Settings ***
2 | Documentation | A test suite with test cases for valet
    parking. |
3
4 | Resource | resource.txt |
5
6 | Suite Setup | Open ParkCalc |
7 | Test Setup | Input Parking Lot | Valet Parking |
8 | Suite Teardown | Close Browser |
9 ...
```

Test cases in Robot Framework are most often defined using a mix of keywords. For some of the Valet Parking examples you can find a set of tests in Listing C.2. This listing shows the contents of one Test Cases section. Please keep in mind that in the setup for each test the Valet Parking lot is picked from the dropdown (see line 7 in Listing C.1). That is why this step is not listed explicitly in the test cases. The three lines in each test case explain what is happening right there.

Listing C.2 A Robot Framework test case section used for the airport parking lot calculator

```
1 ...
2 *** Test Cases ***
3
4 Less Than Five Hours
5 | | Input Entry Date | 05/04/2010 | 12:00 | AM |
6 | | Input Leaving Date | 05/04/2010 | 01:00 | AM |
7 | | Calculated Cost Should Be | $ 12.00 |
8
9 Exactly Five Hours
```

```
10 | | Input Entry Date | 05/04/2010 | 12:34 | AM |
11 | | Input Leaving Date | 05/04/2010 | 05:34 | AM |
12 | | Calculated Cost Should Be | $ 12.00 |
13
14 More Than Five Hours
15 | | Input Entry Date | 05/04/2010 | 12:00 | AM |
16 | | Input Leaving Date | 05/04/2010 | 12:00 | PM |
17 | | Calculated Cost Should Be | $ 18.00 |
18
19 Multiple Days
20 | | Input Entry Date | 05/04/2010 | 12:00 | AM |
21 | | Input Leaving Date | 05/08/2010 | 12:00 | AM |
22 | | Calculated Cost Should Be | $ 72.00 |
```

The three keywords `Input Entry Date`, `Input Leaving Date`, and `Calculated Cost Should Be` are defined in the file resource.txt in the Keywords section. These use lower-level keywords to utilize the Selenium driver and pick the right values in the form. Listing C.3 shows these keywords.

Listing C.3   A Robot Framework keywords section used for the airport parking lot calculator

```
1 *** Keywords ***
2
3 | Open ParkCalc |
4 | | Open Browser | ${PARKCALC URL} | ${BROWSER} |
5 | | Set Selenium Speed | ${DELAY} |
6 | | Title Should Be | ${PAGE_TITLE} |
7
8 | Input Parking Lot | [Arguments] | ${lot} |
9 | | Select From List | ParkingLot | ${lot} |
10
11 | Input Entry Date | [Arguments] | ${date} | ${time} | ${ampm} |
12 | | Input Text | StartingDate | ${date} |
13 | | Input Text | StartingTime | ${time} |
14 | | Select Radio Button | StartingTimeAMPM | ${ampm} |
```

```
15
16 | Input Leaving Date | [Arguments] | ${date} | ${time} |
      ${ampm} |
17 |    | Input Text | LeavingDate | ${date} |
18 |    | Input Text | LeavingTime | ${time} |
19 |    | Select Radio Button | LeavingTimeAMPM | ${ampm} |
20
21 | Calculated Cost Should Be | [Arguments] | ${cost} |
22 |    | Click Button | Submit |
23 |    | ${actual} = | Get Text | ${COST_ITEM} |
24 |    | Log | Actual costs: ${actual} |
25 |    | Page Should Contain | ${cost} |
```

The keywords use variables like $COST_ITEM or $BROWSER. These are
defined in their own section as well. Listing C.4 shows the values for our parking
lot calculator. With Robot Framework you can also override these default values
by providing different values at runtime. You can use command line switches to
pybot to change them. Please consult the user guide on how to do it. There are
multiple ways, and you might prefer one or the other.

Listing C.4 A Robot Framework Variables section used for the airport parking lot
           calculator

```
1 *** Variables ***
2 | ${BROWSER} | firefox |
3 | ${DELAY} | 0 |
4 | ${PARKCALC URL} | http://www.shino.de/parkcalc/ |
5 | ${COST_ITEM} | //tr[td/div[@class='SubHead'] = 'estimated
      Parking costs']/td/span/b |
6 | ${PAGE_TITLE} | Parking Cost Calculator |
```

Since the four tests above use the same three keywords, we could simplify the
tests. Robot Framework provides test templates to achieve this. This is how you can
run data-driven tests from Robot Framework. I extracted a keyword Valet Parking,
which uses the three steps after selecting the Valet Parking lot. This keyword then
takes the entry and leaving date and time as well as the expected costs, and verifies
them. Listing C.5 shows the examples refactored to use test templates. I used
variables to reflect the six different parking durations and give them a more telling
name. Array variables do the trick in Robot Framework.

Listing C.5 A Robot Framework test using a keyword template for data-driven tests

```
1  *** Test Cases ***
2
3  | Valet Parking Test | [Template] | Valet Parking |
4  | | @{FOR_ONE_HOUR} | $ 12.00 |
5  | | @{FOR_FIVE_HOURS} | $ 12.00 |
6  | | @{FOR_ONE_DAY} | $ 18.00 |
7  | | @{FOR_THREE_DAYS} | $ 54.00 |
```

Library Code

Besides the extensive predefined libraries, you might want to come up with code on your own to drive your application. This works similarly as in FitNesse. You basically define a static function in your Python code library that reflects the name of the keyword you are using. Instead of camel-casing the function name, you use underscores in Python. Consult the documentation for library authors[4] for more in-depth examples on this.

---

4. http://robotframework.googlecode.com/hg/doc/python/PythonTutorial.html

References

[Adz09]   Adzic, Gojko. *Bridging the Communication Gap: Specification by Example and Agile Acceptance Testing.* Neuri Limited, 2009. ISBN 9780955683619.

[Adz11]   Adzic, Gojko. *Specification by Example: How Successful Teams Deliver the Right Software.* Manning Publications, 2011. ISBN 9781617290084.

[App11]   Appelo, Jurgen. *Management 3.0: Leading Agile Developers, Developing Agile Leaders (Addison-Wesley Signature Series (Cohn)).* Addison-Wesley, 2011. ISBN 9780321712479.

[Bec02]   Beck, Kent. *Test-Driven Development: By Example.* Addison-Wesley Professional, 2002. ISBN 9780321146533.

[CAH+10]   Chelimsky, David, Astels, Dave, Helmkamp, Bryan, North, Dan, Dennis, Zach, and Hellesoy, Aslak. *The RSpec Book: Behaviour Driven Development with RSpec, Cucumber, and Friends (The Facets of Ruby Series).* Pragmatic Bookshelf, 2010. ISBN 9781934356371.

[Car65]   Carroll, Lewis. *Alice's Adventures in Wonderland and Through the Looking-Glass.* Tribeca Books, 1865. ISBN 9781936594061.

[CG09]   Crispin, Lisa, and Gregory, Janet. *Agile Testing: A Practical Guide for Testers and Agile Teams.* Addison-Wesley, 2009. ISBN 9780321534460.

[Coc06]   Cockburn, Alistair. *Agile Software Development: The Cooperative Game (2nd Edition).* Addison-Wesley, 2006. ISBN 9780321482754.

[Coh04]   Cohn, Mike. *User Stories Applied: For Agile Software Development.* Addison-Wesley, 2004. ISBN 9780321205681.

[Cop04]   Copeland, Lee. *A Practitioner's Guide to Software Test Design.* Artech House, 2004. ISBN 9781580537919.

[dFAdF10]   de Florinier, David, Adzic, Gojko, and de Florinier, Annette. *The Secret Ninja Cucumber Scrolls*, 2010. http://cuke4ninja.com

[DMG07]   Duvall, Paul M., Matyas, Steve, and Glover, Andrew. *Continuous Integration: Improving Software Quality and Reducing Risk.* Addison-Wesley, 2007. ISBN 9780321336385.

[Eva03]   Evans, Eric. *Domain-Driven Design: Tackling Complexity in the Heart of Software.* Addison-Wesley, 2003. ISBN 9780321125217.

[FBB⁺99]   Fowler, Martin, Beck, Kent, Brant, John, Opdyke, William, and Roberts, Don. *Refactoring: Improving the Design of Existing Code.* Addison-Wesley, 1999. ISBN 9780201485677.

[FP09]   Freeman, Steve, and Pryce, Nat. *Growing Object-Oriented Software, Guided by Tests.* Addison-Wesley, 2009. ISBN 9780321503626.

[GHJV94]   Gamma, Erich, Helm, Richard, Johnson, Ralph, and Vlissides, John M. *Design Patterns: Elements of Reusable Object-Oriented Software.* Addison-Wesley, 1994. ISBN 9780201633610.

[GW89]   Gause, Donald C., and Weinberg, Gerald. *Exploring Requirements: Quality Before Design.* Dorset House Publishing Co Inc., U.S., 1989. ISBN 9780932633736.

[HK11]   Heusser, Matthew, and Kulkarni, Govind, editors. *How to Reduce the Cost of Software Testing.* Auerbach, 2011. ISBN 9781439861554.

[HT99]   Hunt, Andrew, and Thomas, David. *The Pragmatic Programmer: From Journeyman to Master.* Addison-Wesley, 1999. ISBN 9780201616224.

[Hun08]   Hunt, Andy. *Pragmatic Thinking and Learning: Refactor Your Wetware (Pragmatic Programmers).* Pragmatic Bookshelf, 2008. ISBN 9781934356050.

[Jon07]   Jones, Capers. *Estimating Software Costs: Bringing Realism to Estimating.* McGraw-Hill Osborne Media, 2nd edition, 2007. ISBN 9780071483001.

[KBP01]   Kaner, Cem, Bach, James, and Pettichord, Bret. *Lessons Learned in Software Testing.* Wiley, 2001. ISBN 9780471081128.

[Ker04]   Kerievsky, Joshua. *Refactoring to Patterns.* Addison-Wesley, 2004. ISBN 9780321213358.

[KFN99]   Kaner, Cem, Falk, Jack, and Nguyen, Hung Q. *Testing Computer Software, 2nd Edition.* Wiley, 2nd edition, 1999. ISBN 9780471358466.

[Mar02]   Martin, Robert C. *Agile Software Development, Principles, Patterns, and Practices.* Prentice Hall, 2002. ISBN 9780135974445.

[Mar03]   Marick, Brian. *My Agile Testing Project,* 2003. http://www.exampler.com/old-blog/2003/08/21/#agile-testing-project-1

[Mar08a]   Martin, Robert C. *Clean Code: A Handbook of Agile Software Craftsmanship*. Prentice Hall, 2008. ISBN 9780132350884.

[Mar08b]   Martin, Robert C. *Fitnesse–The Fully Integrated Standalone Wiki and Acceptance Testing Framework*, 2008. http://www.fitnesse.org

[MC05]   Mugridge, Rick, and Cunningham, Ward. *Fit for Developing Software: Framework for Integrated Tests*. Prentice Hall, 2005. ISBN 9780321269348.

[Mes07]   Meszaros, Gerard. *xUnit Test Patterns: Refactoring Test Code*. Addison-Wesley, 2007. ISBN 9780131495050.

[Nor06]   North, Dan. *Behavior Modification. Better Software Magazine*, 3 2006.

[Tal10]   Taleb, Nassim Nicholas. *The Black Swan: Second Edition: The Impact of the Highly Improbable: With a new section: "On Robustness and Fragility."* Random House Trade Paperbacks, 2010. ISBN 9780812973815.

[Wei86]   Weinberg, Gerald M. *The Secrets of Consulting: A Guide to Giving and Getting Advice Successfully*. Dorset House Publishing, 1986. ISBN 9780932633019.

[Wei91]   Weinberg, Gerald M. *Quality Software Management: Volume 1, Systems Thinking*. Dorset House, 1991. ISBN 9780932633729.

[Wei93]   Weinberg, Gerald M. *Quality Software Management: Volume 2, First-Order Measurement*. Dorset House, 1993. ISBN 9780932633248

[Wei01]   Weinberg, Gerald M. *More Secrets of Consulting: The Consultant's Tool Kit*. Dorset House, 2001. ISBN 9780932633521.

Index

Acceptance test-driven development
 (ATDD)
  collaboration in, 51
  in friendly test automation, 162-66
  gaps in, 149
  successful, 183-85
  support codes and, 49-50, 59-60, 70
  vs. TDD, 118
  test automation and, 162-66
Acceptance test suite, 111-12, 147
Adzic, Gojko, 121, 148, 154-55, 163, 187
Agile-friendly automation, 156, 161, 163,
  177, 178, 193
*Agile Software Development – Patterns,
  Principles, and Practices* (Martin), 124
Agile Testing (Crispin and Gregory), 150
Airport Parking Lot test cases. *See also
  individual headings*
  Automating Remaining Parking Lots test
    case, 41-46
  Parking Cost Calculator Workshop test
    case, 3-15
  Valet Parking Automation test case,
    17-39
Alice's Adventures in Wonderland
  (Carroll), 147
Alpha tests, 150, 151
Appelo, Jurgen, 150
Arrange-Act-Assert format, 136
ArrayFixture, 135
Automating Remaining Parking Lots test
  case, 41-46
  durationMap for, 43-44
  economy parking lot, 44-45
  economy parking lot examples, 44-45
  short-term parking lot, 41-44
  short-term parking lot examples, 41-42

step definitions after generalizing, 42
summary, 46
Automation, 161-68
  collaboration on, 164-66
  domain discovery, 166-67
  domain-specific test language in, 162
  keyword-driven, 137-39
  summary, 167-68
  test, developing, 170-72
  user-friendly, 162-64

Behavior-driven development (BDD), 131,
  132-33, 187
Beta tests, 150, 151
Boundary conditions, 142-43
Boundary values, 144-45
Business-facing tests, 150, 152

CalculateFixture, 134
Camel-casing, 137, 139, 191, 194, 199
Carroll, Lewis, 147
Clean Code (Martin), 170
Clojure, 163
Code. *See also individual codes*
  library, 199
  production, 121-22
  refactoring, 176
  supporting, 59-60
Code in Light States test case, developing,
  66-70
  deciding which one to return based on
    previous state, 69
  final test table for car states, 69
  first example passes, 68
  first flow after implementing light
    configurations, 70
  first support code class, 66

205

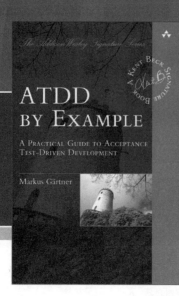

Your purchase of **ATDD by Example** includes access to a free online edition for 45 days through the **Safari Books Online** subscription service. Nearly every Addison-Wesley Professional book is available online through **Safari Books Online**, along with thousands of books and videos from publishers such as Cisco Press, Exam Cram, IBM Press, O'Reilly Media, Prentice Hall, Que, Sams, and VMware Press.

Safari Books Online is a digital library providing searchable, on-demand access to thousands of technology, digital media, and professional development books and videos from leading publishers. With one monthly or yearly subscription price, you get unlimited access to learning tools and information on topics including mobile app and software development, tips and tricks on using your favorite gadgets, networking, project management, graphic design, and much more.

Activate your FREE Online Edition at informit.com/safarifree

STEP 1:   Enter the coupon code: LQMDUWA.

STEP 2:   New Safari users, complete the brief registration form.
          Safari subscribers, just log in.

If you have difficulty registering on Safari or accessing the online edition,
please e-mail customer-service@safaribooksonline.com